CW0670655

Another Dimension ANTHOLOGY

Published by Wily Writers

Another Dimension Anthology

ISBN: 978-1-950427-15-4

(Ingram Spark Edition)

AngelMcCoy.com

in Appreciation...

Behind the Scenes:

Angel Leigh McCoy, Executive Editor
http://www.angelmccoy.com/

Kimberly Michael, Book Design & Typography
http://studiographe.me

Anja Millen, Cover Artwork
https://www.facebook.com/anja.millen.imagery/

We Edit, Content Editors ➭ http://www.editingmckennas.com/

Special thanks to:

Spooked in Seattle Premium Ghost Tour
http://spookedinseattle.com/

Billy Roberts, Paranormal Expert ➭ http://www.billyroberts.co.uk/

Nev Murray, Insightful Reviewer
http://confessionsofareviewer.blogspot.com/

Line Edit Assistance

Bridget McKenna, fiction writer/editor of Aeon Speculative Fiction
Marti McKenna, lead writer at En Masse Entertainment
http://www.editingmckennas.com/

Story Choices by Guest Editors

Alan Baxter, Paranormal fiction author
http://www.alanbaxteronline.com/

Paris Crenshaw, freelance writer, game designer
https://www.facebook.com/pariscrenshaw.writer/

Richard Dansky, author & Central Clancy Writer at Ubisoft
http://www.richarddansky.com/

Kelly Dunn, Horror author ➭ https://kellysdunn.com/

Cory Herndon, lead writer at Carbine Studios
https://www.facebook.com/Cory-J-Herndon-113517064888/

S.P. Miskowski, award-winning Horror author
http://d-o-cat.blogspot.com/

Ripley Patton, YA Paranormal author
http://www.ripleypatton.com/

Loren Rhoads, Horror author and cemetery expert
https://lorenrhoads.com/

*All our friends and family who supported
this project with patience, elbow grease, and love.*

Contents

Fiction

The First Step Into Another Dimension

Tony Albarella

A hearty welcome, friends, to the *Another Dimension* anthology. These pages contain fiction and columns that pay tribute to the genre Rod Serling brought to television in iconic shows such as *The Twilight Zone* and *Night Gallery*. Here you'll find science fiction parables, urban and rural horror stories, and cautionary tales of karmic comeuppance; fantasy both dark and light that runs wild between the extremes of mankind's depravity and the limitless breadth of the human spirit. Many of these shockers will, in true Serling spirit, incorporate elements of social commentary and explore the boundaries of the human condition.

Another Dimension exhibits a focus on examinations of supernatural exploration, of ghosts both physical and emotional, of terror ranging from the brutally realistic to the equally-disturbing variety known as psychological terror. Thematically, this venture recalls for me the excellent newsstand periodical of the Eighties entitled *Rod Serling's The Twilight Zone Magazine*. That publication, expertly edited by Carol Serling as a continuation of her husband's work, highlighted fiction from a wide variety of genre writers, some of whom were newly-discovered talents and went on to highly successful careers. Stylistically and—no pun intended—in spirit, *Another Dimension* also parallels *Rod Serling's The Twilight Zone Magazine* in its reverence for the type of morality tale that Serling mastered. It draws inspiration from supernatural horror and fantasy of the past, tweaks it with a modern spin, and serves it up as a tribute to Serling's legacy.

The very fact that tales of this sort remain in vogue leads to a question that I so often hear: why are supernatural stories so popular? The reasons can be as varied as the tales themselves. Visit a bookstore or library, locate any short story collection of supernatural fiction, and read the introduction. Chances are it will state that ghost stories are as old as fiction itself. Or it will explain the genre's popularity with the theory that tales about life beyond the grave strike directly at some elemental pressure point buried deep within us. Or that our nearly universal fascination with the subject can be traced to a psychological fear of death and the futility of our quest to learn what happens to us after we die. Or, conversely, that tales of the supernatural actually soothe our anxiety about mortality and reassure us with a resolute and emphatic answer to that eternal question, "Is this all there is?"

These declarations exist for one very good reason: they're all true. Supernatural fiction can be laden with subtext for those who wish to analyze and probe for it. And yet, perhaps more importantly, ghost stories are popular because they can be fantastically entertaining. They can lure readers in, dance in their dreams and nightmares. Such stories outlive their creators and, like the very subject they examine, reach up from the grave and out of the past to haunt us.

Supernatural tales run the gamut from children's nursery rhymes to urban legends to centuries-old fiction that withstands intense scholarly analysis—from the Bible to William Shakespeare to Stephen King. The genre can be enjoyed in forms as diverse as supermarket tabloids, comic books, the modern horror bestseller, or classic works from the likes of Edgar Allan Poe, Charles Dickens, Robert Louis Stevenson, Washington Irving, Shirley Jackson, Ambrose Bierce, and Henry James.

When Rod Serling created *The Twilight Zone* and wrote for *Night Gallery*, one of his goals was to tap into the rich literary history of the supernatural and bring it to the small screen. The scripts that were produced for these two series included both original works and adaptations. Some followed the tradition of tall tales told around the campfire; a few were tongue-in-cheek vignettes; but most treated the supernatural theme quite seriously, spinning yarns of spirits that refuse to die, black-magic spells, death incarnate, and intervention by the devil.

English writer M.R. James, widely regarded as a master of supernatural fiction, professed in 1929 that "The sole object of inspiring a pleasing terror in the reader…is the true aim of the ghost story." This description is as apt as any in explaining the success of Serling's groundbreaking television work in the horror and fantasy genres. The creation and presentation of "pleasing terrors" was Rod Serling's stock in trade, and *Another Dimension* strives to pick up that gauntlet for another generation of willing, imaginative readers. From what I've read, the anthology is well on its way to accomplishing that goal.

☞

Fathoms' Embrace

Rena Mason

Xi climbed off her husband, edged over to the bed mat on the floor next to his, then lay on her side and faced the wall. The back of her head tingled in response to the glare she knew emanated from Ming. Not trusting his reaction, she kept one eye open looking up and to the left for anything that might loom toward her.

"We've been married since April of 1903. Almost three years and still you've given me no sons, wretched woman. No children at all!"

"I'm sorry." Any sign of emotion might send him into a rage. If only she were pregnant. His anger and lashing out at her would end the instant he knew. Xi had always wanted to be a mother, but Ming's behavior made her desperate. It had become a matter of life and death.

Hers.

"You should be a lot more sorry. Taking you off your family's hands has brought me nothing but shame. How do you think I look when Lew already has a son and probably another one on the way? My business partner. Bah! We should be equals!"

Xi kept silent, still, braced herself.

"Like a fool!" His fist pounded the floor behind her, and she flinched, held her breath, waited. Not much time went by before she heard him snoring. Could be a trick.

Over the past couple months, she'd allowed Ming to humiliate her sexually, yet it hadn't resulted in a pregnancy. Tomorrow she'd go and see Yan again, the old apothecary on Stockton Street in Portsmouth Plaza. There had to be something the old medicine man could do, perhaps he'd prepare a new elixir. Just about anything would be an improvement compared to the previous crushed dung beetle extract she had to drop on her tongue twice a day. As Xi thought of miracle treatments and cures, she drifted off to sleep, rocked by gentle waves she could neither see nor comprehend.

Ming had left for work before dawn without uttering a sound. Xi listened as he woke and readied himself. She'd kept her eyes closed and her breathing rhythmic, hoping he wouldn't notice she was pretending to be asleep.

After cleaning up and getting dressed, Xi headed toward the center of San Francisco's Chinatown. Salty cold humidity rolled in from the bay and veiled her face in the thin ocean layer she wore almost always, an ever present second skin. The air's salinity dried her pores and made her appearance haggard and leathery.

With so few respectable Chinese women in the city, her family had expected a lot from her looks as a youth. She had been a prize to be had, and Ming, a professional businessman with a metal works factory, had paid them handsomely to have her. But since she'd borne him no children, her family feared what he might do in retaliation, so kept no contact with her—left their most hopeful daughter all alone in an overcrowded place.

Xi stepped into a temple on Sacramento Street and slipped off her shoes, lit a stick of incense, knelt, and prayed hard. Even with determined and loyal supplication her pleas had gone unanswered.

In the darkened silence, gentle lapping waves sounded around her legs. She never thought of herself as a water person, but it called to her as of late.

The pharmacy was a few blocks from the temple. Busy helping a customer at the counter when she entered, Yan looked up over his spectacles at her and shook his head. After finishing the business transaction, the old, hunchbacked apothecary shuffled toward her.

She spoke up after the door closed behind the last patron. "The medicine you gave me didn't work. Is there anything else?"

"You're here almost every week. I've tried everything. It must be your husband. Tell him to come see me."

"No. He won't."

The old man stroked his gray beard. "I understand, Mrs. Li. He's too proud."

Xi lowered her eyes and nodded.

"Hmm…have you thought of other ways to get pregnant?"

"Yes, of course. That's why I'm here."

"But if your husband's body is not in proper alignment, there's nothing you can do."

"Maybe if you give me something for him. I can hide it in his tea or food."

Yan thought for a moment about what she'd said…then spoke. "I'll give you something to try, but if this doesn't work, you should consider seeing someone else to get pregnant."

"Another apothecary, I—"

"No, Mrs. Li." He looked around the empty shop. "Another man," he whispered.

She gasped, stood in shock at his suggestion. The thought had never crossed her mind until then. But should have.

The old man smiled, shuffled back behind the counter and over to the wall of drawers and jars. He selected a few, seemingly at random, then began a preparation.

Xi pondered Yan's idea. Numerous brothels lined the streets of Chinatown. Maybe if she disguised herself and hung around outside one, looking lost or confused, luck would come to her in the guise of a man wanting more than just to be helpful. She could travel across town, avoid places her husband might frequent. It wouldn't be any more degrading than the acts he'd forced upon her recently.

Yan returned with a glass vial and handed it to her. "Put four drops in his food or drink."

"Thank you." She paid him then left with a small smile.

❧

Thoughtlessly meandering through the streets, mulling over the apothecary's alternative suggestion, Xi wound up at the shipping docks. If not for the shrill of seagulls, she might have walked straight off a pier into the ocean. She sat down along an edge of dank boards and looked across the endless body of dark gray.

Halfway out, an opaque wall of fog had merged with the cloudy sky above it and crept toward the city. Winds picked up and gusts blew her tears onto white-capped waves. Xi hadn't even realized she'd been crying. Tears of joy? Resolution?

"Thank you." She spoke down to the water. "Rest only comes when you rock me to sleep, and all I have to give in return are tears. I'm a horrible person."

Ship workers' voices echoed from near and far in the white mist. Then all sound stopped, and a soft, peaceful silence embraced Xi. She opened her mouth and took in a deep breath, tasted the salt. It stung her lungs but something about it felt right. She closed her eyes, inhaled deeply again and again.

"Hey! Move!"

Xi snapped out of her reverie and lurched to the right as something flew mere inches past her shoulder. A dull thud sounded when iron hit the soaked boards next to where she sat.

"What are you doing here?" A man pushing a handcart stepped out of the fog. "You could've been hurt."

Stunned, she looked up at him and admired his handsome face. "Sorry. I came to think, then the weather changed so fast."

"That's how it is by the water. You should be more careful. Can you help me with this?" He leaned down to a small anchor.

"Yes, of course." She stood and grabbed one end. The cold metal bit into her flesh, but she didn't flinch.

"Ready?"

Xi nodded.

"One, two, three, lift." They heaved it back up into the pushcart. "Thanks. It was supposed to be delivered over an hour ago. I should've been more watchful of where I was going, but I was in a hurry. Sorry, I almost ran you over. You were like a ghost in the fog."

She smiled. "No. I'm real. See." Xi bowed.

"My name's Bohai, and I've got to go, but if you're still here on my way back, I'd like to take you for some tea."

"Do you know what time it is?"

"Almost three."

"Oh no, I have to go." She hurried down the pier and heard Bohai shout after her.

"Maybe another time. I'll look for you."

Xi couldn't hide her childish grin as she rushed home thinking that loitering outside brothels might not be necessary with a man like Bohai around. It was possible he knew her husband, but if she met him again in the fog, wore her hair differently, insisted she preferred making love to the sound of waves, he might believe her and agree to a tryst by the sea. Tomorrow held a new hope Xi never thought she'd have again. Her mind meditated on Bohai and how wonderful a pregnancy would be.

But the rest of the day demanded focus. She still had to figure out a way to add the apothecary's fertility concoction to Ming's food. Xi reached into her pocket, took out the small glass vial, and opened it. She bowed her head to have a look and take a whiff. An odorless milky liquid came halfway up the sides. She prayed it had no taste as well.

If her new plan succeeded, she'd have to anger Ming enough to rape her. Avoiding her husband for a day or two usually did the trick. He preferred to take her when he knew she'd cow to him. The most difficult part would be getting him to have normal sex. How did he expect her to get pregnant when he let his seed flow into places where she didn't have any eggs?

Her stomach turned and grumbled at the thought.

Ming hadn't mentioned anything odd about the taste of his dinner the previous night. This pleased Xi, and before going to the docks, she needed to talk with Yu Hong, the pregnant wife of Ming's business partner. It had been weeks since their last visit, that hadn't ended on pleasant terms. Yu should have never suggested that maybe Xi wasn't meant to have children.

Since the Hongs lived across the street from the apothecary's shop, Xi kept her calls to Yu short and somewhat clandestine. She'd never visited them both on the same day.

An expectant Yu answered the door. "Ah, Xi, I'm so happy to see you. Please, come in. I'll get some tea."

Xi nodded, slipped off her shoes, and stepped inside. "Thank you. I'm sorry it's been so long. How have you been?"

Yu walked back into the room carrying a tray, and the women sat down on floor cushions. It took Yu several awkward tries before she got to a position that looked somewhat comfortable.

"I felt bad for what I said the last time." Yu stared into her teacup.

"Please, don't think of it. I've already forgotten what you said."

"It's no one's fault you haven't gotten pregnant, Xi. That's what I meant to say. It just came out wrong. I wish there was something more I could do to help."

"My hope is better now. I feel good changes coming."

"I'm glad to hear you say that. I haven't been feeling so well. This pregnancy feels different."

"What do you mean?"

"I don't know how to explain it. I'm just afraid. I have bad dreams."

"About what?"

"Fire and water. The end of the world. I know it sounds crazy."

"If there's anything I can do, please ask. You've always been a good friend to me."

"Thank you. You're a true friend." Yu looked up at Xi.

Both women nodded, smiled, and sipped their tea.

Xi left worried that something might be wrong with Yu and her unborn child. Even though she couldn't get pregnant, it would break her heart if anything happened to Yu.

She plodded to the shipping docks with her head hung low, glancing up every few feet to look for Bohai. The mere sight of him would surely change her mood. A low fog drizzled moisture onto her clothes and seeped down to her skin. Dank from head to toe, she went pier to pier, but saw no sign of him. She had just decided to head home when he stepped out of the mist pushing an empty cart.

"Ah, good timing," he said. "I just finished my last delivery."

"Why is that good?" Xi used a timid voice and gently brushed strands of wet hair from her face.

"We can have tea now."

"Where?"

"I know a small place, not far from here."

She looked up around for anyone who might recognize her.

As if he knew what she was thinking, Bohai lowered his voice to a soft whisper. "It's very small and quiet. No one hardly goes there. I promise."

Xi nodded, and followed a step or two behind him knowing that her smile beamed, hidden in the salty, wet haze.

She woke a while later, her beaming smile had become a beacon of life—of hope, and a future. Xi knew…felt life growing inside her.

➡

On the night of the third day after sneaking the apothecary's medicine into Ming's food, Xi undressed on her bed mat then crawled over the cool floorboards toward her husband. She straddled him and her long black hair fell around their faces like curtains. Ming had an icy, fierce stare that burned through her. She shuddered, closed her eyes and kissed his lips, worked her way down his body compliantly doing what he'd forced her to do on so many previous occasions.

Pain tore across the top of her scalp, her head jerked back. Ming yanked her off him by a shock of hair, which he then twisted around his hand. He sat upright and tightened his grip, held his other hand up to her face… and in between his thumb and index finger rested the empty vial from the apothecary.

"Whore!" Ming shook Xi's head.

"No. Please. I just want to make you happy."

"It's too late. You think I'm a fool? Yan's been my friend for years. He told me everything!" Ming tugged down hard and knocked her head on the floor again and again.

White stars flared in front of her, then drifted away, fading like fireworks.

She slunk back to her mat, determined to try again tomorrow. It would have to be soon, but afraid of upsetting him any further tonight and unable to put her clothes on, she lay naked on her side and faced the wall, shivering.

Familiar tears and the warm trickle of blood mingled and pooled onto the small pillow. Ming lay behind her on his bed mat, but she didn't hear him snoring. Xi heard nothing at all. She held her breath to listen, her heartrate quickened, and she wanted to look back, but the day's activities had caught up with her. She took a deep breath then exhaled. The rhythmic pattern slowed, and after fluttering her eyelids several times after they'd started to close, she gave up. The gentle rocking waves came to comfort her once more, and Xi fell asleep, unable to keep a watchful eye open.

●

She woke plunging into icy blackness. Her head squeezed as if it might cave in on itself, and she breathed in, coughed and choked, flooding her lungs with seawater. Salt burned and roiled just beneath the skin of her face, behind her nose, and eyes that bulged. The freezing cold tensed every muscle, they screamed with pain. Clenching her fists, she kicked but couldn't move her legs. Xi struggled inside bindings. She fought for life, for the child growing inside her.

Glowing white fog encircled her with the familiar embrace of the sea. Fabric had unfurled from her upper torso and ankles. The ends entwined and floated next to her as they rolled in the billows of an underwater current.

Her last thought became a prayer to Chi Lang, the Seventh Son and demon of vengeance.

Her last glimpse was of his decayed corpse in an ancient body of armor.

"Ming will die." The demon's words were the last she'd ever hear.

Xi accepted that she'd always been a water person, then opened her hands and let go.

⇨

In the House of the Hangman One Does Not Talk of Rope

Gary A. Braunbeck

Alan Westall committed suicide twice before he ate breakfast. The first time came a few moments after he got out of bed; he took the belt from his pants, fastened it securely to the doorknob, twisted it into a tight figure 8, then stuck his neck through the loop and sat down. It took longer than he'd thought it would and was infinitely more painful than he'd imagined, but as he stood watching himself convulse and turn various disgusting colors, he realized that he'd started the day in the best possible manner. He felt much, much better about himself.

After the thrashing and choking stopped, after the final death rattle wheezed from his crushed throat, after his bowels had emptied themselves of their foulness as a final illustration of death's indignity, only then did he take the special container from his pocket, smiling to himself as he unscrewed the cap and heard the faint whoosh-pop!

Empty and ready to be filled.

He took one last look at his body and then ground the flesh and bone under his heels until all that remained was a fine powder, which he carefully scooped up and placed inside the container.

He held it up to the light, studying its contents.

This was, he thought, the Alan Westall who continuously smiled at people he'd rather tell to go fuck themselves. Within the granules was that Alan Westall; the country-club bartender who spent his nights listening to rich, pampered people moan on and on about how their money didn't make them happy, only more privileged and therefore better than the people who served their drinks; better, even, than the families of those who served them with smiling faces. Here was the Alan Westall who felt like a whore every time he collected his paycheck—and a cheap one, at that. Because he served the rich and privileged, and they were the ones who'd shut down the plant where his father had worked for over thirty years, and Dad started drinking then because he was fifty-eight years old and no one would hire him and there wasn't enough money because he'd been sixteen months short for his pension and there was no way that Alan Westall could make it better and now both his parents were dead, rotting six feet under, killed by poverty and frustration, beaten to death by a world they never harmed. And so their surviving son was a whore.

Or had been, rather.

Now he was dust.

The new Alan Westall smiled, slipped the container into his pocket, and went into the bathroom to shave. He had just applied the shaving cream and opened the straight-razor when the phone rang. The old Alan would have cursed, then stormed into the middle room to answer it, but the new and improved Alan Westall had a better attitude, and so smiled broadly. Nothing could faze him now. He answered the phone, not minding at all the shaving cream he smeared on the handset.

"Hel-loooooo," he said cheerfully.

"Hi'ya." It was Janet. "So...I guess you're still alive after all, huh?"

"So it would seem."

"Listen, I was just going through some stuff and found a couple of your books." She read the titles. He couldn't remember any of them.

"You can keep them," he said.

"I figured you'd say something like that."

Something of the old Alan stirred within him. He didn't like the taste it left in his mouth. "Let's not argue anymore, okay?"

"No, of course not. In order to argue we'd actually have to be talking to one another, wouldn't we?"

"I'm not sure I follow."

"Jesus, Alan! You haven't so much as called me in almost three weeks! The last time you spent the weekend, you hardly said a word. Then you just disappeared. I think you owe me an explanation and an apology."

"Why were you going through things?"

Janet gave a disgusted sigh. "Because I'm moving, that's why. A senior copywriter position opened up at a branch office in New York and they offered me the position."

He felt nothing, though he knew he should have. "Well...I guess congratulations are in order."

"I didn't call to...goddammit, I didn't call for you to bestow accolades on me, I called because I..." She fell silent. Something of the old Alan stirring told him that she was desperately hurt, and he should try to do something to make up for it.

He waged a fierce battle in the silence and lost.

"You can keep the books to remember me by. The good times, anyway."

"Ask me not to go."

"W-what?"

"Ask me not to go, Alan. Tell me you're sorry about pulling another one of your disappearing acts, tell me that you're back in therapy and want to get over your depression about your parents, tell me that you'll try harder not to be in a fog most of the time. Please? Tell me that the ugliness is over and everything will be fine between us from now on—Christ! At least ask me to help you. You've never done that, you know? I don't know if it's that annoying Midwest blue-collar work ethic or just some bullshit macho streak in you, but you've never once asked me to help you through any of this. I will, I swear to you. Just say the word and I'll turn down the position, tell them I've changed my mind. They told me I could. They hate the idea of losing me here so it's not like I'd be screwing myself out of a livelihood. All you have to do is give me a little something, Alan; all you have to do is ask."

He tried in the silence and couldn't do it.

"I hope you like it in the Big Apple."

A wet, spluttering sound from her end. "Oh, God. Why can't you let it go? None of it was your fault, but you have to put yourself on the rack over it, don't you? You had no idea your father was capable of something like that. How...how could you?"

"If I'd been paying more attention, if I'd cared a little more, I would have seen it coming."

"Don't say that! It isn't true and you know it as well as I do! You spend so much time brooding over what you should have seen, or did, or noticed, or realized, or whatever in the hell it is you chastise yourself for constantly, that you don't see the things you can do something about. Why is it that people are precious to you only after they're a memory?"

He felt the shaving cream run down his neck, saw it drip onto the floor, soaking into the carpet. "Be happy, Janet. And find someone who'll love you well." He didn't wait for a reply; he hung up, disconnected the phone, walked into the bathroom, picked up the straight-razor, and stared at the reflection staring back at him from the mirror—some man who had once been a boy, and was not what the boy had once dreamed of becoming.

He sneered at the face.

You should call her right back, you know that, don't you? Call her back and beg her to forgive you and stay. But you won't. Why is that, you suppose?

Part of the old Alan was still in that face that stared back at him. Deceptive bastard that he was. And that was the part that had hung up on Janet. That was the part that had just driven away the best thing that ever happened to him. Kind, caring, intelligent and articulate, perceptive, everything the boy had once dreamed of finding in a life-mate, silenced forever by the simple act of yanking a cord from a wall.

Now there was no one for him.

The face reflected at him didn't deserve anyone.

And so Alan Westall took his life a second time by inserting the tip of the razor into the base of his forearm and pulling it up to the wrist, opening his flesh like the pink maw of some loathsome insect, watching as the blood slopped out into the sink. Ignoring the pain, he did the same to his other arm, then stood back and watched as he collapsed against the bathtub, arms extended, staining the white porcelain.

He felt no sympathy for the pathetic creature huddled before him. It deserved to die a coward's death, alone and cold and filled with misery. No sympathy at all.

When it was finally done, when the thing before him was elbow-deep in its own gore, Alan removed the container, unscrewed the cap—pop-whoosh! —and ground the body into dust, then scooped it into the container, mixing it with the powder from earlier. Then he was on his knees, can of cleanser in hand, washing out the tub until it was restored to its original shiny white. Then he cleaned the sink. Then he shaved. When his face was smooth and clean he saw that he didn't quite recognize the man who stared back at him, but felt as if he could learn to like this man a great deal.

And so to the kitchen to prepare breakfast for this new friend, this better friend, this one-and-only best friend who was now the only one he had.

While the English muffin was toasting, he sat down at the table with his cup of black coffee and picked up the yellowing newspaper page, the same page he'd read every morning for the last six months, and looked at the small headline over the article three-quarters of the way down:

MAN KILLS WIFE, SELF

As always, his eyes began to tear.

He took the container out of his pocket, unscrewed the lid—pop-whoosh! —and poured the powder into his coffee, turning it a deep, rich butterscotch color.

Not minding the searing pain in his throat, he drank it down.
Felt something old and familiar fill him to the brim.
And wondered how many times he'd die before supper.

Stones

Brad Ellison

The smell of the eviscerated fox, ripped body left out in the sweltering heat as it had been, was overpowering. The stink of it filled the damp still air long before he saw the thing.

Looking at it didn't make it any better.

It was coming on noon now, and he'd been hiking through this overgrown old trail since the sun came up. Hot sweat glued his backpack to him, and his camera strap had rubbed a raw spot on his neck. He felt like he was drowning in a steaming cauldron, and his hair was plastered damply to his head, the sweat dripping down his neck and leaving furrows in the dust on his skin.

And now here he was, in the middle of a long-forgotten trail, face to face with this brown fox that was staring up at him with one milky eye. The other, being popped a little way out of the contorted skull, was aimed towards the creature's left hind leg, which looked to have been torn off and tossed to one side. The innards had been opened up and spread out some, ripped at but not eaten. Ants and maggots had begun their work on the remains, their swarming making the corpse ripple unwholesomely.

Drips of dried blood led from the reeking carcass to a stone on the side of the trail. It was a chunk of granite, roughly squarish and about a foot tall and long and wide. It was much weathered, but he thought he could make out tool marks on it, as though it had been chiseled off of a larger stone at some point.

Atop the stone sat the fox's liver.

It had rotted some, like the rest of the body, but there were no insects working on it. It lay bare and untouched on the stone.

His guts twisted. The smell filled him—his nostrils, his lungs, his body and his brain. He thought of himself breathing in that decay, letting it flow through his bloodstream, and then sweating it out, hot salty drops of perspiration beading out of his skin, all smelling of rot and death.

He held his breath, and walked as wide around the dead fox as he could, on the side of the trail opposite that bloody stone.

He had no appetite, but he needed a rest. After putting some distance between himself and the carcass, he began looking for a good spot to stop. He considered an old log on the side of the trail, but when he probed it with his toe he disturbed the horde of ants within the rotting wood, and he remembered the shifting mass that coated the fox's guts, and thought better of it.

It was about fifteen minutes later that he came to a clearing.

The thick brush that had hemmed him in fell away. This open space was not large, perhaps half an acre at the most, but after the closeness of the dense trail, its width gave him a little shock of vertigo. Without the closely woven canopy of tree limbs overhead, the direct midday sun came down on him like a hammer, and the air he breathed in felt like steam.

There was a house in the middle of the clearing. A small ramshackle structure, old and tired, whatever paint it had worn long since peeled off, and the wood cracked and splintering. It leaned drunkenly to the side; the empty door and window frames slanted at an unhealthy angle, as hollow and black as the eyes of a skull. An ancient pile of rust that had been a screen door lay in the weeds as did a number of old wooden shingles and the remains of a tin rain gutter. The roof was sagging in, and had holes in it. The place looked like it had stood empty since the end of Prohibition.

About halfway between the house and the edge of the clearing, there was a large slab of dark granite under the shade of an old oak, the only tree inside the clearing. A bit over six feet long, perhaps three or four wide, and two deep, the slab put him in mind of a coffin. It occurred to him that this stone matched the one where the fox lay.

Beyond that slab, to the side and a bit back from the ruined house, he saw five grave stones, of the same dark granite.

He tensed, feeling keenly aware of everything morbid in the scene before him. Paranoid dread made him think of being watched by hidden eyes.

But the summertime noon was too bright and too hot for the feeling to last, and he was too tired to hold onto tension. He stepped forward to the bare gray stone. Under the spreading branches, the air was more bearable. The rock itself, he found, was cool to the touch.

He sat in the shade, making himself comfortable and splashing his face, neck and wrists with water, thirstily drinking. The buzzing of the mosquitoes was mesmerizing, and his mind drifted as his body cooled.

Before long, his appetite returned, and he put his attention to one of the sandwiches from his pack.

As he ate, he looked at the graves, wondering who was buried there, where they'd come from, and how they came to be here. When the sandwich was gone he stood, picked up his camera and walked over to them. He'd come out for pictures of nature, but here was strange history, a novel outcropping of the past breaking into his day, and he wanted to record it.

One stone was older than the others, more worn, though it was of the same matter and bore similar tool marks, as though chiseled by the same strong hand. It stood apart, the grave it memorialized choked with thick weeds, and cut into its surface, deep and sure, were the words:

OBEDIAH WRIGHT

1893

WATCHING AND WAITING FOR US

He frowned. He'd seen such epitaphs before, in old cemeteries, like the quiet Colonial section of the Rhode Island graveyard where his father had been buried a few years ago. A promise of reunion in the world to come, on the markers of pious Puritans. There was something sinister about the sentiment, coupled as it was with the newer graves that showed the promise fulfilled in the dirt beneath his feet.

Those four were more uniform in appearance and free of weeds. Nothing grew from the naked ground in front of them. Their inscriptions looked to have been done by the same hand, in the same unadorned style.

ISAAC WRIGHT

1913

EASTER

SARA WRIGHT

1913

CHRISTMAS

ROBERT WRIGHT

1914

EASTER

ELIZABETH WRIGHT

1914

CHRISTMAS

He shuddered. What had happened here?

He looked at the house, and again he shivered at how the slouched door looked like an open mouth. But his curiosity was aroused.

He crossed the field, grass and weeds rustling beneath his feet, climbed the sagging front steps, and walked inside.

☛

The kitchen was first. The floor was simple wood planks, warped and rotted and treacherous. A few scraps of faded wallpaper Hung halfheartedly like a leper's skin. It was all dilapidated: a rusted wood-burning stove, a splintered table in the corner, and three chairs reduced to cracked sticks. A few pages of a Montgomery Ward catalog succumbed to mildew on the glass-strewn counter next to a shattered window. Two or three chipped plates sat on a shelf. It all smelled of decay and long disuse.

He picked his way across the floor to the door leading further into the house. The doorknob was a corroded lump that would never turn again, but the door was ajar, and the hinges swung easily enough, though not without noise.

The next room was dominated by a grandfather clock. The works were spread across the floor in front of the case. Nearby was an old armchair that stank powerfully of mold. There was another little stove here, a pot-bellied shell of rusty iron half collapsed in on itself.

There was only one window in the room, narrow and shuttered. The slats were broken, and when he went to look through the gap they left in the shutter, he could see the oldest grave, standing silently with its shadow pointing towards the house like a stubby finger.

He turned away and noticed a narrow high shelf built into the wall by the window. There were three objects on it, all covered in a thick layer of dust: a book, a mallet, and a large chisel.

Dust swirled up as he picked up the book, and he held his breath. Under the dust was fine leather and gilt-edged paper. A family Bible. Opening it to the middle, he saw that there were pages missing throughout the volume, including what seemed to be most of the Psalms, the entirety of the gospels, and the first and last chapters of the Book of Revelation. Some passages had been underscored in heavy black ink, seemingly at random. In Isaiah's twentieth chapter, every instance of the word "the" was underscored, and every occurrence of "God" was crossed out with a heavy hand that bled through to the underlying page. In the Book of Hebrews, the name "Rahab" was circled at the heart of a spiral that covered both pages in tight counterclockwise loops. The story of Samson killing with a jawbone was thoroughly underlined, right before a series of missing pages that spanned through to the story of David and Goliath, which was similarly underlined.

He turned to the front of the disfigured book, hoping to find a genealogy or other family records. It seemed that there had once been a family tree, but it was mostly torn away. A surviving scrap of paper bore the words Obadiah Wright, married Sa--.

Next to this was an old and brittle photograph, tucked between the leaves. A grim-looking man with a heavily lined face and large powerful hands stood before a wagon, flanked by children, two on his left, three on his right. The oldest was a boy who looked to be in his mid teens. The youngest was a girl in pigtails, holding a rag doll. In the wagon, he saw what looked like a large slab of dark stone, about eight feet long.

On the back of the photograph was an inscription, in a spidery hand. It said simply "Wright family, St. Louis, 1891."

He returned the picture to its place and put down the Bible.

Looking at the hammer and chisel, he suddenly felt sure that they would be cold to the touch, handles sticky, and that under the dust the blade of the chisel would be bright, clean, and sharp. He suddenly felt aware of the fact that he was trespassing in an abandoned house far from any outpost of civilization. In his mind's eye, he saw that chisel flash and carve those recurring holidays into granite markers. In his mind's eye, he saw the chisel drip blood as it cut into the stone.

Who were these people, and what had happened to them? Why?

☛

By the time he stepped out of the ruined house, it was later than he had realized. The shadows of those five grave markers were lengthening, stretching out toward the granite slab like dark fingers. Their darkness served to make the brightness of the afternoon sun more sharply apparent. It was hotter than ever, the air thicker. He grasped his camera—feeling the device slip in his dripping palms like it was trying to escape him—and snapped a picture of the graves and another of the stone, and then turned to take one of the house.

When his back was to the granite slab, he felt, as clearly as an itch between his shoulder blades, the dead certainty that he was being watched.

His finger slipped away from the button, and he knew, absolutely knew, that there were eyes on him, that someone was sitting on the slab of granite, staring at his back.

It took forever for him to muster the courage to turn around, but the horror of being crept up on from behind was even greater than the horror of seeing his fears confirmed. He was trembling and dripping sweat as he finally cast a glance backwards.

No one. No trace of a human presence.

Not even the trail he'd followed.

The buzzing of the mosquitoes was gone. The world had gone still, and the silence was such that his quickening pulse began to deafen him.

He went stiff, every muscle tense, heart racing and blood pounding in his ears. Beads of sweat dripped from his nose and stung his nostrils.

He still felt eyes, but was certain they were peering out at him from a window now. He could picture it clearly, that deep-lined solemn face from the photograph, with those broad hands tightening on the chisel.

His throat tightened,cutting his breath short. He whipped his head around, trying to turn in every direction at once. He spun in place, then paced back and forth around the stone, his hands starting to shake. No trail, not in any direction.

Where did I come from then? Nowhere? Get a grip, get a hold of yourself, you've gone a long time without a panic attack, breathe, count, there's no one watching you.

He forced himself to suck in a deep ragged breath and stared at the ground in front of him trying to remember the calming exercises that had gotten him through those bad years at college after his dad had died.

On the ground in front of him, there was another shadow next to his.

He turned and saw nothing behind him. He looked back, and saw the second shadow still stretched out next to his own.

He heard a whimpering sound and realized it was coming from his own throat. He fell to his knees.

The panic lasted forever. At the end of it he was panting, gasping, feeling weak, sick and utterly exhausted.

The other shadow was gone. There couldn't have been another shadow. Couldn't have been. The mosquitoes were buzzing again.

So tired. Not since school. None that bad since…Tired.

He got up and staggered to the sanctuary of that spreading oak, sat on the cool granite, and felt the tension drain away as if leeched by the stone. The buzzing was hypnotic.

He hardly knew what he was doing as he stretched out.

☛

He dreamed blood. He dreamed flashing blade, hammer thud, and stone chips flying as headstones were born from the rock, the names running crimson as the bloodied chisel scribed them. Even in the dream he was afraid, but in his dream, he understood why it had to be. The hunger of the stone, needing to be fed. The communion of those given into it, whatever was left of them remaining a part of the stone forever. This was an honor, a calling to a higher purpose.

When he woke, that higher purpose, that why, was gone.

The sun was just an orange glow along the top of the tree line now. Long shadows swallowed him, skeletal tree and grasping tombstones, hungry monstrous house. They had all melted into one great web of darkness and eaten the day.

In the distance, he heard the mournful cry of a whippoorwill. And then it too was gone.

Much closer, he heard the sound of a chisel biting into the stone, shaping the newest marker.

Kit Power

For Jason, it was love at first sight.

"Mummy! Ted!"

Snatching him out of the gutter. Holding him up to her. Excited. En-raptured. Caz had seen that look enough times to know what it meant.

She regarded Ted wearily. The 'fur' was a dirty dishcloth grey that made her want to wash her hands just looking at it. His eyes were crude stitches of dark blue thread—vacant Xs. The nose was a loosely thread-ed button that might well have come from the cardigan of an aged child molester (and was, in Caz's opinion, practically a dictionary illustration of 'choke hazard'). The belly sagged unpleasantly, like the beer gut on a wife beater. There was the faintest waft of mould.

There was no polite way to say it: Ted was hideous. Hideous enough that it actually took a little effort for her to turn her gaze to Jason. His little face excited beyond all reason, eyes shining with happiness, with the warmth of true love, pure and complete and possessing as only a toddler can feel.

Ah, crap.

Caz thought about resisting. She thought long and hard, because she really didn't like the look of Ted. At all. But she could visualise with perfect clarity the scene that would unfold if she did—the tears, the tantrum, and worst of all the incessant screaming. Just the effort of thinking about it wore her out.

Screw it. Let him keep it.

"Ted looks like he needs a wash, don't you think?"

"Ted!"

"Yes, Ted looks dirty! Shall we wash him when we get home?"

With bleach. Or fire for preference.

"Ted! Home!"

"Yes, yes, we'll take Ted home and give him a wash, OK?"

"Ted!"

With the tired and heartfelt sigh that is the universal signal of maternal surrender, Caz took Jason's free hand and continued walking home.

"Ted!"

❧

"Ted!"

Jason's face was red now, angry.

"Yes, sweetheart, Ted needs to go in the washing machine. He's dirty and Mummy needs to clean him."

"Ted!"

Eyes narrowed, nostrils flaring, mouth a thin angry slash. So much like his father in his rage, Caz thought for the millionth time, hating Jason just a little, in the moment, for the reminder. Hating herself for the reaction. The old, dull, helpless despair came flooding back as it had so often in the months since Andy cut and ran, threatening to sweep her away, drown her.

But here was Jason, dragging her back. As he always did. Her sweet, sweet boy.

"Jason, Ted needs a clean, that's all. You can see him, here"—tapping the glass door of the washing machine—"he'll be OK. It's like Ted having a bath! It'll be fun for him!"

"No! Ted!"

Clutching the bear tight, hugging him protectively. Caz recognised the futility of what she was trying to do—reason with a two year old; might as well try and win an argument with a brick—and snapped.

"Give me the bloody thing!" Snatching, grasping hard, tugging. Jason was standing in front of her, arms crossed over Ted's stomach, so she was left grabbing at one of those misshapen, stubby legs. As her grip tightened, she felt its contents shift and grind together, like sand or pebbles. The texture of his skin was clammy and faintly nauseating. Still she tightened her grip, meaning to tug him out of her son's grasp.

"NO!" Hysterical, furious, Jason struck out at his mother's face with all the strength in his two-year-old body. Hard enough to hurt. Hard enough to bring a tear to her eye and more than hard enough to cause her to drop Ted's leg in shock.

He ran from the room immediately, sobbing but not wailing, still defiant and angry. Caz stayed on her knees, staring at the open doorway, the hand that had clutched Ted's leg now tracing the shape of the blow on her cheek. More tears fell then, and she let them. Kneeling on the kitchen floor, she wept bitter tears of hopelessness and rage and frustrated, trapped love. The tears pooled on the cheap linoleum and soaked into her jeans.

☞

The day passed as they do. Jason watched TV, played with his trucks and cars, ate, had his nappy changed. He laughed and cried and belched and farted. The only difference was his new constant companion. Ted stayed by his side, paw crushed into Jason's right hand. Caz recalled the dank feeling of the fur, the weird texture of the stuffing, and wondered how Jason could stand it. But there it was.

With each new activity she thought Jason would finally need both hands and release Ted, but he did not. It got so she almost suspected that Jason could read her mind, knew she wanted to separate them (only to clean the damn thing, for crying out loud) and would not allow it to happen. Then she remembered a simple truth: he was a two year old—and stubborn as only a two year old could be—and the thought relaxed her.

☞

Come bath time, Caz had simply assumed that Jason would give up Ted easily enough. Not a bit of it.

"No! Ted!"

She saw the look in his eye, felt a tingle on her face where he had struck her before, and immediately decided not to push it. Forget it. Let him take Ted in the bath. Let him take the damn thing to bed if he wanted to. Once he was asleep, she could retrieve the godforsaken thing easily enough and clean him.

Or, you know, get rid of him. It.

"Okay, Jason, okay. But you have to get undressed, okay?"

Jason immediately swapped Ted to his left hand and held his arm out for her to pull the sleeve of his jumper.

Cute.

In this way, she undressed him, Ted swapping from hand to hand, Jason's grip firm, unrelenting. She was sure he'd get dropped in the bath, but no. Jason sat in the tub with one hand out over the edge, dangling Ted above the bathroom floor while his mother washed him. Caz ignored this as best she could, but couldn't help stealing glances at Ted, swinging to and fro. His distended belly. His blank, expressionless face. Twisting.

"Up. Please. Mummy!"

"Good boy! Milk time?"

"Milk! Teevee!"

Some things don't change, she reflected with a smile. She lifted Jason from the bath and into a radiator-warmed towel.

Jason curled up on the sofa and drank his milk just like always, watching his usual bedtime programme with heavy eyes. He acquiesced willingly enough to his mother putting on his pyjamas and brushing his wet hair, though the dressing followed the same routine as the undressing had, with Ted moving from hand to hand in constant contact. Caz observed this with frustration but no real surprise. It was okay. Jason would be asleep soon enough.

Some things didn't change.

Sure enough, his eyes glazed...went half-lidded...then closed. He continued to work the bottle in his sleep, and Caz watched this very ordinary miracle with the same overwhelming wave of love it always engendered. Jason. Her little man. She placed her hand gently on his chest, feeling his breathing, his heartbeat. Remembering when that heart beat inside her. His jaws slowed and finally stopped working the bottle.

Gone.

She kept her hand there a while longer, enjoying his warmth and the rhythm of his sleeping body. Gradually, her gaze turned to his hand, still gripping the arm of that grotty little bear.

Ted.

He—it—was face down on the sofa, which was a mercy. But even the sight of his mangy 'fur' gave her a frisson of disgust almost strong enough to make her shudder.

Christ, that thing was ugly.

She reached for it, then hesitated, remembering the feel of that skin and its contents. She did not want to touch it again, she realised. Quite powerfully did not, in point of fact. Still, Jason had clearly fixated, so that was that. But at the very least...

"At the very least, you, my furry little friend, are having a bloody bath."

Unaware that she'd spoken aloud, she reached for Ted and gripped his midsection. The 'fur' still had a damp and somehow warm feel, like that of a dog with a fever. Worse, as her fingers began to sink into what she found herself thinking of—with rising disgust—as his flesh, she felt again the sensation of near-solid objects moving and grinding beneath her grip. The sensation was exquisitely unpleasant and she wondered how Jason could possibly stand it. Still, she got enough of a hold to pull.

Jason's eyes flew open immediately, his free hand tugging the bottle from his mouth. Caz jerked back in surprise and fear, releasing Ted and rocking backward.

"No, Mum. Ted. Bed."

Not angry this time, thank God. Not angry, but firm just the same. Certain. Cold? Caz let out her breath with a bark that was not quite a laugh and not quite a sob, but could have been either. Or both.

"Okay, Jason, okay, don't worry. I'm not gonna take him. Bed time?"

"Bed."

"Okay."

She picked him up and carried him up the stairs, heart hammering unpleasantly against her ribs. Jason's anger had been one thing, but this...calm certainty—so outside his usual nature—was something else. Up until that moment, Caz's feelings on the subject of Ted had been merely displeasure and contempt. This was the first moment she'd felt fear. The taste was bitter.

Well, screw it. Just screw it, that's all. She'd put Jason in the cot, then just take the damn thing. He could scream and cry all he wanted - scream the bloody house down - she was taking that bear and he was going in the bloody rubbish bin and that'd be the end of it. That second touch had convinced her, even before her son had woken up to command her in that calm, cold voice. Ted was bad fucking news and Ted was not welcome in her home.

But when they got to Jason's bedroom, her son did something totally unexpected - he gave Ted up as easy as pie. Just as she went to lay him down in the cot, he got his legs under him and stood, holding Ted out to her.

"Ted. Mum."

"You... you want me to take Ted? Mummy take Ted?"

"Yeh."

Okay.

She reached into the cot, and Jason released him without a moment's hesitation. The sensation of discomfort at holding the thing was still there, but Caz barely noticed, so powerful was her relief (and deeper, her gratitude) at her son's sudden change.

Jason pointed to the corner of the room.

"Ted."

Caz sighed. So close... but, ah well, still an improvement. Ted wasn't in the cot, and there'd been no bedtime screaming fit. Most important, Jason had given him up. Could she stand to leave him in the room? She was relieved to discover that she could, under the circumstances. Ted could sit in the corner tonight and take a late night bath once Jason was asleep. Hell, she could probably have him dry and back in place by the morning. The worst of her boy's possessive fever had apparently broken and all else could be forgiven, negotiated.

"You want Ted to sit in the corner?"

"Yeh."

"All right."

She carried him—it—over to the corner of the room, next to the radiator and sat him there, facing the crib.

"There. Okay?"

"Yeh."

Sleepy. Lying down.

"Good. Ted still needs a bath though, okay?"

"Yeh."

"All right, we'll do that tomorrow then, yes?"

"Yeh."

Half-asleep already. Drifting. She crossed back to the cot.

"I love you Jason. I love you so, so much. Sleep tight, little man. See you in the morning." She leant in, kissed his forehead, tousled his hair gently, and left the room, turning off the light on her way out.

❧

Her intention was to put Ted through the washing machine that evening, but intentions are poor and fleeting things. The wave of relief at Jason's change of heart carried her to the bottle of wine in the kitchen, then the TV called her to the sofa with the promise of her soap opera, then a movie she really liked. Somewhere around her second glass, she felt the tension of the day evaporate in the warming, numbing glow, and by her fourth glass, she'd forgotten Ted had ever existed.

She made her way slowly and a little unsteadily up the stairs, brushed her teeth, and all but fell into bed. Two minutes after her head hit the pillow, she was snoring deeply.

❧

In her dream, Jason was crying. Great, lusty cries of pain and fear. She was in a gigantic house, a mansion, full of long corridors and doors. She ran down the corridors, flinging open door after door, running into room after room, all huge, all identical, all empty. His screams seemed to be coming from everywhere and nowhere, and with each empty room, her own terror increased, until she sprang awake, drenched in sweat, yelling.

"Jason!"

Her heart beat fast and hard, her mind still trying to shake the horrible vividness of the dream. Then her brain caught up with the frantic signal from her ears. The crying hadn't stopped—was, in fact, rising in pitch and volume. Hysterical. Agonised.

Muscles locked, screamed, flung her out of bed as if on wires, propelling her with such force towards her bedroom door that she collided with it, bounced back even as her hand dove for the handle.

An incoherent prayer tumbling from her lips, unknown and unheard, her hands tore the door open with such force that it rebounded and smacked her hard on the shoulder as she passed through it, oblivious to the injury and the pain, indifferent to anything but the screams of her son. Screams that were losing their urgency, becoming muffled.

Becoming faint.

She flung open his bedroom door as the final scream ended on an impossibly high note, abruptly cut off, and she knew, with a cold finality, that she was too late, even as the prayer continued to babble, and her hand scrabbled like an injured spider for the light switch.

The light flashed on, flooding the room with awful, harsh light, obliterating shadow. Ted lay in the corner, now just a curled ball of dead skin. His face gazed at the ceiling and two dark, moving trails led from his lifeless, crude eyes.

In those last precious seconds of lucidity, her eyes sent her mind images it could not process, leaving her to see without comprehension. The trails were seething, boiling, rippling. As she followed their movement, head turning slowly (too slowly) towards the cot, her gaze began to pick out the individual creatures, crawling over each other: shining black bodies, carapaces like beetles, but leaner, more like ants, tumbling and scrabbling over one another in their eager progress.

The trails parted at the bars of the crib before closing again, becoming a writhing, roiling black blanket. Her head continued to turn, so slowly, already feeling like an automatic, uncontrollable action, eyes rolling in their sockets, somewhere deep down a voice saying don't look don't look don't look don't look don't. But still her head turned, still her eyes refused to close. The dark swarm covered a bulge exactly the size and shape of her infant son. His legs, torso, chest—all swaddled in the chittering, consuming darkness, shining and simmering like a layer of tar. The understanding lurked, pregnant, on the edge of her consciousness, and still her eyes moved.

Until they came to rest on his face.

There she observed with perfect clarity the bleached white paleness of his skin, his eyes wide, sightless, vacant, gone, mouth thrown open, cheeks stretched taut in a frozen mask of agony and terror. Still screaming that final, soundless cry.

The moment held, unwound. Her last second of conscious thought unspooling, stretching, becoming thin. Eyes and heart and mind pulled past breaking point by that awful, pleading face.

Then the creatures, burrowing from beneath, boiled up out of his mouth and across his face, consuming, devouring, with an awful scraping, grinding, cracking noise, like boots marching over gravel, and the shape of his body began to sink, becoming indistinct.

Collapsing.

Comprehension dawned, finally—a thermonuclear sun, a wave of total destruction that obliterated her conscious mind with awful, devastating mercy.

Her now-unseeing eyes remained there until the creatures, summoned by her smell and the promise of fresh meat, crawled up and over her face and ate them from their sockets.

Ted fed.

☞

On Rod Serling's "Clean Kills and Other Trophies"

S. T. Joshi

Rod Serling's television series *Night Gallery* (1970–73) tends to be regarded as something of an embarrassment, even among Serling devotees. In a documentary that accompanied the boxed DVD set of the complete *Twilight Zone*, "Rod Serling: Submitted for Your Approval" (originally shown on PBS's American Masters series), the three-year-long run of *Night Gallery* was covered in a matter of seconds, as an utterly forgettable episode in Serling's later career.

In some senses, this disdain is warranted. *Night Gallery* was clearly not the groundbreaking, even revolutionary show that *Twilight Zone* was; and because Serling did not have full editorial control over the series, he felt unable to stamp it with his unique moral vision. As he noted to Universal Studios: "I wanted a series with distinction, with episodes that said something; I have no interest in a series which is purely and uniquely suspenseful but totally uncommentative on anything."

But on the upside, *Night Gallery* did present some vivid and memorable episodes (in living color, no less), including adaptations of several classic weird tales—H. P. Lovecraft's "Cool Air" and "Pickman's Model," stories by August Derleth and Basil Copper, and an unforgettable adaptation of Conrad Aiken's "Silent Snow, Secret Snow."

But it is one of Serling's own teleplays—"Clean Kills and Other Trophies"—that I wish to discuss here. In particular, it is worth comparing it with the short story that Serling subsequently wrote based upon the teleplay. Serling wrote two slim volumes of *Night Gallery* stories (1971, 1972), paralleling the three equally slim *Twilight Zone* books he had written earlier (1960–62). As we compare the teleplay with the story, we see how radically Serling could revise the basic thrust of an episode to create a very different moral and psychological effect.

"Clean Kills and Other Trophies" aired on January 6, 1971. It featured a bluff, dogmatic, and intolerant elderly man, Colonel Archie Dittman, Sr. (Raymond Massey), an enthusiast of big-game hunting—and, by extension, a proponent of a vicious "survival of the fittest" morality—who holds his apparently spineless and cowardly son, Archie Jr., in extreme contempt. Accordingly, he makes a curious stipulation before Archie Jr. can secure the millions of dollars that would come to him from a trust upon his twenty-first birthday: he must kill an animal with a gun. Archie Jr. (Barry Brown) seems resigned to carrying out the demand, although the family lawyer, Jeffrey Pierce (Tom Troupe), objects. Archie Jr. accompanies his father on a hunting trip and manages to kill a deer, although it is not a "clean kill" because the animal was shot in the lungs and lingered for hours before dying. A surprise twist occurs when the Colonel's African manservant, Tom Mboya (Herbert Jefferson Jr.), subsequently summons his tribal gods, who apparently behead the Colonel so that Tom can mount the head on the wall of a vast room in the house containing the heads or bodies of the many other animals the Colonel has killed over a lifetime.

The episode is moderately effective because of the taut conflict between the Colonel and Pierce, and because of the brooding presence of Tom Mboya, who appears on the surface civilized but continues to be under the sway of the "savage" gods of Africa.

What Serling did in writing the story was to cut the figure of Tom Mboya out of the scenario altogether. In the teleplay, Tom at one point prevents Archie Jr. from recklessly shooting his own father on the stairs of his house (not out of sympathy for the Colonel, as we learn later, but only so that he himself can gain his supernatural revenge on him). This scene is eliminated entirely—or, rather, is transferred to the end of the story, where Archie Jr. kills his father with the very gun he used to shoot the deer. Archie Jr. tells Pierce (who, in contrast to the teleplay, had accompanied the two men on the hunt) that it was "An altogether clean kill, Mr. Pierce. A damned clean kill."

Serling was shrewd in eliminating the Tom Mboya character. The central conflict in the scenario is that between the Colonel and his son, and the figure of Tom proves to be a somewhat distracting character. The logic of the story requires that Archie Jr. be the one who causes the Colonel's death as a way of both physically and morally declaring his independence from him and asserting his own individuality. Also, the teleplay's O. Henry-like supernatural ending is a trifle contrived (as well as being telegraphed well before it is revealed to the viewer); in the story Serling drops it and produces a chilling tale of psychological terror and suspense where the son's vengeance on the father is carried out without any adventitious use of the supernatural.

The story, of course, also allows for numerous characteristic rhetorical flourishes that make Serling's short fiction a pleasure to read. Whereas in the teleplay the Colonel's intolerance and overt racism are conveyed by his condescending treatment of Tom Mboya (and this, in fact, may be the central reason why that character exists at all) and in other relatively innocuous remarks, in the story Serling does not hesitate to put the pejorative word "nigger" into the Colonel's mouth on several occasions, as an unmistakable marker of the Colonel's vicious prejudice. Later in the story, the Colonel refers to his son as "a nutless, faggoty, simpering little son of a bitch who dishonors me"—another remark that Serling could probably not have gotten away with on a show on broadcast television.

In the story, the Colonel waxes eloquent about his impressive gun collection in such a way that one comes to believe that this obsession with guns verges on the pathological. And Serling writes pungently of Archie Jr. after the Colonel lays down his stipulation about killing an animal: "A birthright was being stripped from him like an animal pelt." (Both the teleplay and the story have the Colonel state: "Didn't Adam Smith have a theory about overpopulation?" This is of course an error, for it was Thomas Malthus who made such a theory in his *Essay on the Principle of Population* [1798]. It is not clear whether this is the Colonel's error or Serling's.)

The story "Clean Kills and Other Trophies" is one of Serling's best—featuring crisply realized characters, a prose style laced with sardonic touches, and, most importantly, a firm moral vision that condemns the savagery of the "kill or be killed" (im)morality advocated by the Colonel. Serling was plagued with doubts about his abilities as a short story writer; but his entire output, and this story in particular, shows that he easily deserves a high rank among the weird fiction writers of his time.

☞

Awesome Justin

Patrick Walters

Three young women huddle under blue club lights. The trio have their lips protruded and flattened. Justin swipes his thumb upward. Mom posted a status. He skips this one too. "Thirty one movies that will make even the manliest man turn into a little girl." He opens it for later.

Some distant noise calls out.

A man and woman are kissing in a park's grassy clearing on a beautiful day. They are engaged. Justin "likes" it.

"The bread is really good."

Bread? "You'll never believe Denise's amazing comeback." He opens it.

"Hey. Are you there?" asks a feminine voice. His neck is itchy. He scratches it.

To himself, he reads, "I don't care what Crystal says, her p-"

"Justin, put it away," the woman, his girlfriend Natalie, demands.

"Alright, alright. But let's take a selfie first," Justin patronizes. He squeezes into the booth beside her just long enough for them to make cute faces, hers nearly overshadowed with irritation. As soon as he snaps the photo, he's back to his side of the table, and she pushes her puckered lips to the side as she rolls her eyes. The human face is a small thing, but subtle variations in its landscape can reveal the world to those who look upon it. Justin's eyes are on his screen, examining Natalie's joyful façade from a moment ago. Her eyes are half-closed, but he himself looks adorable. He crops her out and posts the photo online. He puts the phone away.

"So this bread is good?" asks Justin, brushing open the folded cloth napkin to take a roll from the basket.

"Yes."

"What's wrong? I put it away."

"Nothing. You're right," she forces herself to agree. "You have to use the butter."

He slices off a sizable chunk of butter with a knife. His phone vibrates. He instinctively sets the bread down. She's watching him. He picks the bread back up, butters it, and takes a bite. He emphatically announces its deliciousness, and she smiles. His phone vibrates again. He smiles back.

☛

"I've really got to go to the restroom." She says the words he has been waiting for.

Before she can stand up, his phone is out of his pocket, and he's eyeing the nine total notifications from various social media platforms. Several people liked his photo. One even commented on his cuteness. Another person invited him to something. He responds to the girl who called him cute. When he returns to his news page, he is confronted with the recommended page "follow" of a woman of the most perfect example of beauty he's ever seen. Her name is Kate Sinclair. As he explores her photos, the front of his pants grows tight, and a little bit of drool runs down his chin. A woman, his girlfriend Natalie, says, "Sorry-"

He jumps, wipes his chin, and says, "God! You scared me!"

"Why? What were you looking at?" she says with an accusing laugh."

He had already impulsively shut his phone off. He looks at the black screen and wipes his eyes. He takes in a deep breath and says, "It's a little embarrassing, but I think I was just about to fall asleep."

"What? Really?"

He yawns. He has been able to yawn on command since he was seven or eight. "Yeah. I don't know what's wrong with me. I guess I just need some sleep."

She offers, "Hell yeah, you do. I've never seen someone fall asleep at dinner before. We don't need to watch a movie tonight. You can just take me home."

"It's OK," he says. "I'll be fine. We can watch a…" He yawns.

"No. We can watch it another time. You get some sleep."

☛

Upon arriving home, he goes to his bedroom. He takes off his pants and opens his laptop to visit Kate Sinclair's page. She has hundreds of thousands of followers, but she has never done anything special. She's never publically sung a song or played an instrument. She doesn't act. She's never written a book. The only picture of her doing charity work is from a mandatory high school event. She is just an awesome person. He sticks a hand in his boxers. His phone vibrates. It's Natalie. He flips the phone over, concealing the flashing notification light.

A few weeks later, Justin is uploading a picture on his laptop when he gets a phone call. He answers it, and his dad says, "Are you free this evening? Your mom wants you to join us for dinner."

Justin looks at the screen in front of him. His video of him dancing at a club receives another comment as his dad waits for his response. Justin's already substantial amounts of "followers," "friends," "admirers," and "fans" have all tripled over the past few weeks. He suddenly has the strong urge to post a witty status. He responds, "Sorry, Dad. I'm busy tonight."

"Alright. Soon then?"

"Soon," he confirms. He's checking the new message.

"Talk to you later."

"Later." He begins rereading through the nearly one hundred and fifty comments from friends and strangers complimenting his dance moves, face, and clothes. He shuts his eyes and begins to take a deep breath, but it is cut short by another phone call. It's Natalie. He answers. She is angry about how little time they have spent together lately. While they talk, he scratches his itchy head, and gets a notification. Kate Sinclair has commented on his video. She says, "These guys did a hilarious version of the Wombo dance!!! Check them out!!" He tells Natalie that he is sorry, but he has to meet his parents that evening and hangs up.

He places his hands on his keyboard and begins contemplating how he'll respond. Some black residue is stuck under a few of his nails. Is it dirt? He hasn't been outside. He tries to dig it out with a clean nail. It's more gelatinous and adhesive than dirt. He rolls it into a ball, flicks it away, and starts typing his response to Kate. It goes, "Wow, this is so amazing, i never expected someone like you to see this video, thank you so much for sharing it!!!"

Five minutes pass. Kate responds, "It was awesome! Keep it up!"

His insides go soft with success. His head itches, and he scratches it. When he brings his sticky fingers back down, he sees a few strands of hair. Instantly, he gets four comments on his video. His insides burn with success. The likes keep ticking, and he leans back with a grin, deciding to send Kate a private message.

"Why do you want to take me to dinner?" That is Kate's first riddle.

He doesn't know the answer, but he types, "why does any guy? to get to know you."

"Do you know how many guys ask me out weekly? What makes you different?"

"i don't know to explain it, but i feel we would connect on a deeper level."

"After one conversation?"

"trust me, just give me a chance."

"Trust you? I don't know you. Prove it to me."

He looks outside. The sun has set. Night feels darker than usual. Maybe the streetlights are out. He notices a dull hunger that feels like the quiet sounds of someone screaming far away. Perhaps his stomach disappeared with the sun. He stands and immediately collapses to the floor. His legs have fallen asleep. When he finally makes it to the kitchen, he grabs a sandwich and a Coke and heads back to his room.

Upon entering his room, he heads straight toward his blinking phone, and just before grabbing it, he freezes. On the screen are three black smudges that resemble the gunk he found under his nails. He plucks a few tissues from a box and uses them to wipe the phone clean. He sits down, and before he can check the phone notifications, he is met with the waiting conversation window on his laptop screen. How can he prove it to Kate?

He writes, "i would break up with my girlfriend for you."

"For one date?"

"for several dates." He takes a bite of his sandwich. It soothes his itchy tongue.

"Why?"

"i want to be with you." A distant hunger rejoices at a chewed gift of turkey, bread, and cheese.

"Is there room?"

"i told you i would break up with her for you." Justin takes a sip of the Coke.

"That's not what I mean."

"what do you mean? my parents? my friends?" It rains somewhere. Someone rejoices.

She doesn't reply.

He rubs his eyes. The laptop screen is bright. He offers, "i don't need them."

She responds, "OK. Let's meet. Bring her with you."

❧

The weathered wooden door scratches his knuckles as he knocks. The exterior of the large house is not well kept. Justin struggles to see the house Kate had been standing in front of in the online photos. The lawn is plagued with ivy, and the white paint around the windows has molded to a blotchy gray. He looks back at his car. Natalie's asleep in the front. He knocks harder, and an automated voice announces, "Please come in."

He pushes the door open. Dust lines everything inside. The only light is that which makes it through the foggy windows from the dwindling, evening sun. The house is big enough for a family but tranquil enough to have had ample time to adapt to its absence. A gently curved flight of stairs descends to kiss the dark, hardwood floors of the entranceway, and a corridor underneath the hooked arch branches off in many directions as revealed by dim patches of sunlight. His bottom itches. He scratches it. A framed photograph resting on a piece of furniture beside the door displays Kate, her parents, and her younger brother. The electronic voice croaks, "I'm upstairs. Before we go, I want to show you something."

When he is at the top of the stairs, the voice instructs, "Turn left, and I'll be behind the third door."

The hallway is dark, but the frame of one of the doors on the left emits a sterile, electric blue. His fingertips itch, so he scratches them. Something is curled into a ball at the end of the hallway. It sparkles like a sleeping, black dog sprinkled with ice crystals on a cold night. It might be breathing or maybe that's just Justin. When he is upon the door, he slips, barely catching himself on the door knob. The blue light illuminates the dark liquid on the wooden floor. He tries to sniff the air, but his nose is stopped up. The voice speaks, "Before you enter. Tell me. Are you only in to me for my appearance?"

Justin thinks for a moment, rubbing his tired eyes. A hungry man somewhere in the world is starving. He concentrates on his stomach. The sun has taken it. He clears his throat, and says, "I told you. We connect. I feel we have a connection."

"What connection is that?" asks the robotic female voice.

Justin opens his mouth. Some saliva thick like honey drips onto his chin. He says, "Together we can be the biggest social media stars of all time. Don't you feel it?"

"Come in," she says with delighted surprise.

His hands tremble even though his heart doesn't. He squeezes the doorknob. Its metallic surface isn't cool or warm. It's an extension of the air, but it's denser. He turns it and pushes the door open. His left leg falls asleep. He is met with the whirring of electronics and the sight of an expansive display of monitors against the opposite wall. Behind them is a wide, black window. Night has fallen, a thick, dark night like a wall, but the wall is not painted black, rather it is the essence of black. No light reflects. Outside of the window exists nothing. In front of the screens is a large dark office chair. Behind him is the sound of light footsteps. He begins, "What are-"

"Don't be afraid. To achieve the glory you seek, this is the logical next step," she announces.

Three of his profile pages appear on the screen. His followers and friend requests have multiplied ten times each. He scratches his head even though it doesn't itch. The female voice says, "As you can see, I've helped you out."

Dozens of photos and witty comments that he never posted pelt the screens. He asks, "How? I… I never even took these photos."

"If you stay with me, you too can share my power: the power to post anything your mind can imagine, the power to be the perfect social media figure," the female voice says, Kate says. The voice is Kate. She is awesome. Justin will soon be awesome too.

"I will stay with you," he says.

"Then tell me not what you would do for me, but what you would do for yourself," Kate Sinclair says, and the chair turns to face him. In it is a white humanoid figure with no legs, eyes, ears, nose or mouth. From the bottom of the torso extend a thick mass of cords that spread throughout the room into the various electronic devices. The being's eyes are craters that are filled with the same porcelain skin that stretches across its entire body. The nose is a thin ridge, and the lips have grown together. From the fingertips extend frayed wires. Justin cowers, and something heavy slides through the dark hallway behind him. A woman is screaming. Rays of blue light wrap around his shoulders from one of the other rooms, but darkness quickly overcomes it once again. The screaming stops.

Kate Sinclair, the awesome abomination, asks, "What would you do for yourself?"

"I would kill," he responds.

"Anyone who stands in our way? Could you kill your boring mother and father, selfish friends, or your nagging girlfriend?"

Justin searches his memory, but he can't recall any of those people. He scratches his head. It feels soft. One of his fingers gets stuck in his scalp, and he pulls it away. The skin on his head tears, but he feels no pain. He says, "For global fame and love? Yes."

"In that case, I must tell you that something is about to happen. I-"

"Why would I rule with you when I could have all the glory to myself, you ugly bitch?"

"What are you saying?" asks perfectly flustered Kate Sinclair.

"The power is in your computer, isn't it? Why do I need you?" he asks as he leaps upon her. His tingling hands wrap around the soft white neck, and the windpipe crushes under his grip. Kate's atrophied arms can't repel his assault. Despite her caved in throat, the female voice yells, "Hurry!"

Justin feels the mass of cables under his shins, and begins yanking them out of her body. With a pop from each knot of cords, an inky-black stream of viscous liquid seeps out. As the last one is torn from her, Kate asks, "Where am I? Who are you?" and then lets out a gargled combination of a scream and television static. He hurls the mutated corpse out of the chair and sits in the puddle of putrid black fluid. Reveling at the sight of his new-found collection of admirers, he begins typing his responses. The chords on the floor begin snaking around his legs, and from his frayed fingertips extend thin wires. The screens start fading, and his mind slips in and out of time. Comments, images, responses, and videos all coalesce into a con-glomeration of feelings and reactions. Everything makes sense. He creates who he is. He is who he creates. The sun didn't take anything. He gave it all to the sun. Somewhere in the distance a woman says, "My, my Justin, what have you done?"

"Who's that?" Justin, awesome Justin, mumbles through his tight lips. The voice belongs to someone he was once close to, but it is tainted by Kate's sexiness.

"You don't recognize me? C'mon baby, you really need to stop turning me down from dates."

"Natalie?" His whole body itches. The room grows darker.

"Unfortunately, yes. How did you ever give it to a girl with the body of a plank? Thank God for plastic surgery."

"Kate?" screams Justin, but to him, it sounds like a mumble.

"Thanks for a human body, sweetheart."

Something in the room purrs with the crackle of electricity or is it snow crystals clinging to a loyal, black dog? Kate tenderly says, "Thanks to this idiot, you almost didn't hook her up in time. Who's a good little brother? There's your reward."

Justin can feel the electromagnetic presence linger to collect some-thing and then leave the room. Justin then sees the reflection of his own quickly mutating face in one of the screens. He waves his arms aimlessly, mumbling a barely audible, "You can keep her body. I don't care. But, why would you do this to me?"

He feels a tug on one of the wires in his legs, and a sharp pain shoots through his entire system. The woman says, "Not like I can give it back now. The plan was to keep her as my slave, not kill her. You know? Have the best of both worlds. Whatever. You got what you wanted. You loved me because you wanted to be me and now you are. Hell if I'm going back to that though. Together you and I will be famous forever. You go ahead and get to work on updating my new profile. I'm going out."

His mind is instantly flooded with images of his own new profile. If he had a mouth he would smile. Somewhere in the world, two parents lose a child and friends lose a friend or maybe they lost him long ago.

☞

The Children's Song

```
MEMORANDUM FOR RECORD
    #
    Name: Jonas Regan
    Rank: Private First Class (E-3), United States Army
    Date: 22 October 2012
    Subject: Official Report from the Last Known Survivor
    of the Siege on Combat Outpost (COP) Rapier in Pak-
    tika, Afghanistan
    #
    Sir/Ma'am,
    #
```

I've been ordered to write this report about what happened during the siege on COP Rapier, and how my entire platoon could have been wiped out in a matter of days. Twenty nine men removed from the earth. Except for me, of course.

I'll admit that I considered lying. The truth will almost certainly send me to prison if anyone believes it. But I need someone on the outside to do something for me, and that can only happen if I tell the truth. Prison can't be as bad as where I've come from.

First, let me give my condolences to the families of Private Michael (Mickey) Barlow, my platoon mate, and Sergeant First Class Bobby Borderham, my Platoon Sergeant. As the only other survivors of the siege, and my friends, I was saddened to hear they lost their lives just when they were finally free.

I was told to describe events as completely as possible. To that end, please assume the words "shit" and "fuck", and variations thereof, appear roughly once per sentence in this memo, and every other word for patches of dialogue that I recall, to get the complete effect.

Anyway, the siege. I'll start at the point where the public record ends and mine begins. Here's the timeline.

\#

`20 September:`

\#

My platoon on the day we were flown into COP Rapier: Jindo (platoon commander), Borderham (platoon sergeant), Chutes (squad leader), DeShawn (squad leader), Wilson (medic), Hash (forward observer), North (radio-telephone operator), Regan (me), Barlow, Estevez, Julius, Smith, Lowman, Court, Ombad, Locross, Mather, Lyles, Bell, Yowman, Lewis, Quinto, Wiess, Abrams, Steward, Zapato, Delores, Spendolish, Kane.

\#

(There were 42 of us when our deployment began about 16 months ago: three killed in action, four injuries, five mental breakdowns, one suicide.)

\#

Rapier is in the middle of nowhere, even by Afghan standards. No roads in or out. Nestled in an arid glen, it's only accessible via Chinooks or by foot. No running water or electricity, either. The COP was a joint Afghan National Police and US Army training base, but the training mission was cancelled and the COP scheduled for demolition after the Afghans started shooting their US trainers in the back.

Half a dozen Afghan policemen staggered out of a dull brick bunker to greet us. Since I was the resident platoon interpreter ("good with language", my military instructors noted in my training report), they gave me a rundown of the outpost that I passed on to the platoon headquarters, and in less than an hour they'd loaded their stuff onto the Chinook we'd come in on and were gone.

Our orders were to keep Rapier out of enemy hands until allied civil engineers could tear it down. Protect the hole in the ground until it literally became a hole in the ground. And what a hole it was. Two bunkers, including the one the Afghans had come out of, were the only livable quarters on the outpost. The bodies of four other buildings rotted on the northern end, their floors used as impromptu latrines even though the sliced oil drum that served as the COP's official latrine was only two-thirds full. In front of those buildings was a single mortar pit, and in the center of it all was a torn volleyball net. Besides my platoon, the COP's only defenses were four Mine-Resistant Ambush Protected (MRAP) vehicles that'd been left behind by the Army trainers. Home sweet home.

Our commander, First Lieutenant Lars Jindo, wouldn't tell us how long we had to be there. Lieutenant Jindo was like that. He probably didn't know how long we'd be there, but he masked his ignorance with accusations of insubordination towards anyone who asked questions. Behind his back we called him "Captain Ahab" because he was forever chasing the "brown whale" that blew off part of his foot with an IED during his previous tour. If he couldn't find his brown whale, then any brown whale would do.

Honestly, we didn't mind the camp as much as we should have. Our tour was over in two months. If all we had to do was squat in this camp and kick sand around until then, it would be the best two months of our tour.

\#

21-24 September:

\#

Uneventful, for the most part, though Barlow complained to Estevez that he was hearing strange noises from the surrounding hills during his night patrols. Barlow told Estevez because Estevez was our de facto spiritual advisor, and Estevez told me because he was my best friend.

Estevez was Catholic, real religious. Loved God and Jesus and all that stuff, but like a real man should—with compassion. I consider myself generically Christian, in that I believe in the Christian God, but I've never been a regular churchgoer or prayed for anything that wasn't out of desperation, and the same went for most of the guys in my platoon. But towards the end when the macho bravado and patriotic sense of purpose wore off, he was there for us, promising God loved us despite the things we'd done.

Strange how people will only touch each other under specific circumstances. Many nights ago, after Lieutenant Jindo had ordered the platoon to burn down an Afghan village for possibly harboring insurgents, I was overpowered by the need for real human contact, flesh on flesh. As I lied in my sleeping bag next to Estevez, I asked him to hold my hand, and he did.

Estevez told me that Barlow had heard something—a mix of chattering and humming, a noise that was just out of focus, the kind you hear traces of when the din surrounds you but disappears when confronted by silence. No one else heard it.

\#

25 September:

\#

Barlow complained again about the noise, but this time Smith and Abrams backed him up. There was talk about mentioning it to Lieutenant Jindo, but vetoed on account of Private Shotters. Five months beforehand, Shotters had complained about bug bites. The medic gave him a clean bill of health, but he still scratched himself like a kid with chicken pox. Finally

Lieutenant Jindo made him strip naked and had every platoon member inspect him for bites. A couple weeks later Borderham caught Shotters literally eating bullets, swallowing them like communion wafers. For luck, he said. He got sent home the next day. Shotters' brain was shot, Lieutenant Jindo had laughed. Haha.

The strange noises went unreported.

The day was uneventful until night fell. From nowhere, a volley of rockets struck the COP (where the volleyball net was) and instantly killed Yowman and Julius, and seriously wounded Weiss and Court.

Arms and legs blown off, charred flesh.

We ran around like ants whose hill had been kicked, until those of us not already on patrol converged in the bunker. The whiskey, Wilson, worked furiously to stabilize Weiss and Court, applying tourniquets to Weiss's missing arm and Court's missing leg and forearm while they screamed, not out of pain but out of desperation. How badly they wanted to live. No matter how many times you hear it, you never get used to it.

North, the comms guy, tried to radio in a call for immediate air assistance and medical evacuation. No response. The communications equipment wasn't working. North couldn't fix it, because he didn't know what was wrong with it.

Wilson said the injured men wouldn't last long outside of a hospital. We had two options: wait for whatever was wrong with the equipment to resolve itself, or use one of our four MRAPs to send someone for help in lieu of using it to defend the COP. After urging from Borderham, Lieutenant Jindo made the call to send the MRAP for help.

He assigned Ombad and Locross to haul ass to Forward Operating Base Munoz, about fifty miles to the north, and pray they didn't hit an IED or get stuck on the rocky terrain. It was probably the most important mission they'd ever had. They swore they wouldn't fail.

I watched them drive away, swallowed by the night. That was the last time anyone ever saw Ombad and Locross.

The commander then organized the platoon for a search and destroy mission. According to Hash, the rockets had come from the eastern hills. We thought we could flush them out despite blackness in every direction. Chutes, the only rifle squad leader in our platoon (the other two had died months before—no replacements), led two squads up the hill while the weapon squad brought up the rear. The weapon squad shot two rockets into the hills—BOOM BOOM—and peppered the crest with machine gun fire while the two rifle squads swarmed upward, ready to shoot anything that moved.

Big booms and machine guns are usually enough to make most enemies flee, but on this occasion we were met with heavy gunfire—so heavy that it was clear after about thirty seconds that we were outgunned, at least to the east. Chutes ordered the squads to fall back and move south, then head back east for the flank. But an onslaught of bullets met us to the south, and the north, and the west.

Surrounded.

Chutes ordered the platoon to fall back to the COP as bullets poured over us. From what I could see and what I was told after the fact: Smith was shot in the face—he was dead by the time he hit the ground; Mather was shot in the neck—he ran for a while before he collapsed and thrashed on the ground until he finally died; Lyles was shot in the leg—it must have hit an artery because blood spurted everywhere as he shrieked for help. I grabbed his coat collar and dragged him as far as I could until I was shot in my left hand. Estevez helped me get him the rest of the way to COP Rapier. Lyles' eyes were empty by the time we pulled him to safety.

Disarray. Quinto and Abrams were also shot. The whiskey tried (unsuccessfully) to keep them from bleeding to death while the less seriously injured tended to each other.

It was then that we all heard it, without a doubt. The mystery noise in the hills. It was the sound of crying children.

\#

26 September:

\#

My platoon at this point: Jindo (platoon commander), Borderham (platoon sergeant), Chutes (squad leader), DeShawn (squad leader), Wilson (medic), Hash (forward observer), North (radio-telephone operator), Regan (me), Barlow, Estevez, Julius, Smith, Lowman, Court, Ombad, Locross, Mather, Lyles, Bell, Yowman, Lewis, Quinto, Wiess, Abrams, Steward, Zapato, Delores, Spendolish, Kane

\#

The crying continued into the day, coming from the hills, from all directions. The comms equipment was still down. North theorized that our attackers had set up a series of loudspeakers beyond our line of sight and were playing the horrible crying noise on a loop. Delores thought they'd recruited children and forced them to shoot guns and cry. Lieutenant Jindo told Hash to find out where the damn noise was coming from so we could shut it the hell up.

Hash snuck down a crack between the eastern and southern hills, blending into the terrain like a trout at the bottom of a muddy lake. He'd stop, lift his head ever so slightly to survey the landscape, inch forward, stop, etc. We'd watched him leave, but after a few minutes even we couldn't tell where he was anymore.

Not until a sniper's bullet jerked him backwards like he'd been upper-cut by a prizefighter.

Lieutenant Jindo immediately ordered us to fire on the hills in front of Hash with the MRAP grenade launchers, though we knew the range on the launchers wasn't far enough to reach whatever was behind the hills. But Lieutenant Jindo was in a rage, we were in a rage, so we fired everything we had at those goddamn hills.

Eventually we ran out of grenades, but the crying didn't stop. The voices of weeping children ricocheted off the walls and filled every part of the COP. Even with hands over your ears, you could still hear them. Children crying for food. Children crying in pain. Children crying for their mothers. Unrelenting.

We did this. Bowman was the first to say it. God is punishing us. Silence choked the platoon as we considered the truth. We all looked at Estevez; he rubbed his chest where his cross was nestled underneath his shirt, and shook his head.

God would not be this cruel, Estevez said. We wanted to believe him.

Captain Ahab barked at us to stop yapping about superstitious crap, that our invisible attackers were real, that they were messing with us because that's what those tribal bastards do. He swore we'd wipe their genome from the face of the earth.

About this time, Wilson reported that Weiss and Court had died.

Lieutenant Jindo threw down his cover and ordered the platoon to prepare for another assault. Borderham cautioned against it; the wind was picking up and the air was getting dirty. A dust storm was on the way, and we still had no idea where the attackers actually were.

Did you not hear what I said, or are you questioning my orders? Lieutenant Jindo got up in Borderham's face as we watched, frozen.

We will not let them go. We will kill every last one of them, Captain Ahab told Borderham. They were a hair's width from coming to blows. Borderham backed down from the officer, like he always did, but his eyes promised consequences.

The wind was whipping hard by the time we'd donned our gear and mapped the plan of attack. Dust slammed us from every angle. Images devolved into static at more than two arm-lengths away. But we had unity of purpose. Purity of conviction. I think. That's what we were supposed to feel, anyway. All I felt was fear.

The platoon split into three teams and stormed the eastern hill, two teams on opposite sides and another down the middle, to box them in and force them backwards. The teams' instructions were to stay in single-file lines so we didn't lose sight of each other.

We ran into the storm, hoo-rah-ing over the children's cries until our voices were hoarse.

Somewhere halfway up the hill I heard screaming. Men's screams. Kane stopped in front of me, his face white. Lewis and Zapato practically ran into me from behind, surprised by the sudden halt. Kane had lost sight of Chutes, said a monster had dragged Chutes away. He pressed his hands to his ears, eyes wild. Shut up, he screamed at the wailing children. Shut up shut up shut up shut up shut up shut up shut –

Out of the corner of my eye I saw something, a black thing, moving through the storm. Just as I turned to look at it, it swept forward and yanked Kane out of sight as he shrieked and clawed at the air. I stumbled backwards and landed on my back. The upside-down figures of Lewis and Zapato sprinted away in a panic.

Gunfire, sporadic and close. More screaming, desperate pleas for help, too many, in too many directions. Fall back, someone yelled, fall back.

I rolled over and scooted on my belly back down the hill until the ground flattened. I sprang up and made a mad dash back to where I thought the COP was, zigzagging until I ran into a wall and followed it back to the front entrance.

A few of the attacking platoon were already there. Estevez scrambled to staunch the blood flow from an eight-inch slice in Bell's chest while Bell's eyes rolled back into his head. Barlow paced in a circle and pawed at the bloody smear where his right ear used to be. Moments later, Lieutenant Jindo and Borderham burst through the front gate, dragging an unresponsive DeShawn with them. They laid DeShawn on the ground and screamed for the medic to do something about the gaping wound in DeShawn's neck. The medic hadn't come back.

No one else came back.

\#

27 September:

\#

My platoon at this point: Jindo (platoon commander), Borderham (platoon sergeant), Chutes (squad leader), DeShawn (squad leader), Wilson (medic), Hash (forward observer), North (radio-telephone operator), Regan (me),

Barlow, Estevez, Julius, Smith, Lowman, Court, Ombad, Locross, Mather, Lyles, Bell, Yowman, Lewis, Quinto, Wiess, Abrams, Steward, Zapato, Delores, Spendolish, Kane

#

I think it was technically the next day, anyway, very early morning on 27 September.

I was doing something—I don't know what—when I saw a green aura, a point in the distance distilled by the dirty air like a flashlight through frosted glass. Maybe a portal to Hell had opened over there, the mouth of the underworld gaping to let its demons pour forth. That would be the logical thing to think at this point. Instead I thought of a book I'd been forced to read in high school, The Great Gatsby, and the green light at the end of the dock that Gatsby was always coveting but never reaching. Something about the illusory nature of the American dream. And I couldn't believe I thought of that, of all things, like maybe I could have gone to college and been an English major, instead of here. The thought made me laugh. I laughed so hard I cried.

Then I was in a chair in one of the bunkers (don't remember how I got there), Estevez and Barlow beside me, watching Lieutenant Jindo line up all our guns and remaining weapons on a plastic table while Borderham told him he was out of his mind.

We need to prepare for another assault, Lieutenant Jindo said. We are the United States Army, the best fighting force in the world. We do not give up.

Borderham slammed his hands down on the table. Do these men look able to fight? We are not your kill squad any longer. It's over.

It is not over. It is never over. They will pay for what they've done.

You did this, Borderham said to Captain Ahab. You brought them here. It was you.

They stared at each other, like they did before, but this time it was Lieutenant Jindo who turned away, to give us a rousing speech, the first one he'd ever attempted. It went something like this:

"When we signed up to serve our country, we knew we'd have to fight. We knew we might die."

Behind Lieutenant Jindo, Borderham clanks the guns around, inspecting them. The commander ignores him. He picks up an unloaded 9 mm pistol.

"This is the time when we have to stand tall, stand together, to avenge our fallen brothers."

Borderham slaps a magazine into the pistol.

"I know you guys are scared. I know you guys are tired. But we're all that's left."

Borderham racks the slide back, loads a round into the chamber. Estevez clutches the cross of his necklace and mumbles a prayer in Spanish.

"We need to finish the mission. It's time to man up, for America."

Borderham points the gun at the back of Captain Ahab's head. Barlow cries softly. I stare stupidly. None of us says anything.

"And if we die then at least we die as soldiers—"

Boom.

Borderham laid the gun down and sat with us. He patted Barlow on the back, there there, child. Barlow cupped his hand over his good ear to keep the children's cries out. Then Borderham began to sing the Caisson Song; it drowned out the cries. Then he sang America the Beautiful, and we joined him. Then we sang the National Anthem, then the Marines' Hymn, then Hey Jude, Sweet Caroline, Danny Boy, Mary Jane's Last Dance, Sweet Child O' Mine, Paint It Black, etc. We sang all night, every song we knew, even the stupid ones, until the night retreated.

I don't know when it happened—or I guess stopped happening—but when we'd finally ran out of songs, when our bodies were husks and our throats were sandpaper, we realized the crying had stopped.

We walked outside into clear air and a gentle breeze. The sun floated above the horizon. The hills around the COP were quiet, peaceful. Borderham ran off to check on the comm equipment (would turn out it was working again, and he'd finally get a distress signal through). Barlow lay down on the ground, flat on his back, closed his eyes and passed out.

Estevez and I walked just past the front gate and surveyed the desolate landscape. We were so alone, we might as well have been the last two people on earth. This time he reached for my good hand, and I gave it to him, like he'd done for me countless times before. Then he said goodbye, released my hand and walked away, up the hill, over the crest and out of sight.

#

And that's what happened. You know the part about Borderham dying in a helicopter crash on his way back to the States, and Barlow hanging from a bed sheet in the closet of his childhood home.

As for Estevez, I haven't seen him since, and I don't know where he went. He just walked away—away from COP Rapier, away from the war, away from the God that abandoned him. I figure he walked to the end of the world and jumped.

This is what I need: if you look for him, and you find him, please tell him to come back to me.

#

END OF REPORT

➱

Larry Hinkle

Eighteen hours ago, approximately 72 hours after the incident started, every camera in the lab had gone dark. But not before giving the President one last glance into Brundle's upper chamber. He replayed the final few minutes of footage on the monitor above his desk.

The ceiling of the facility's upper level was between thirty and forty feet high in spots, blasted out of the rock itself. Dozens of creatures flew between the steel support beams, diving and swooping between power cables, knocking out lights with a flick of their spiny, whip-like tails. Human-shaped cocoons hung from the rafters. The President didn't want to know what was in them.

Or why some were still moving.

*

"What did the President know and when did he know it?"

Any time a hint of scandal made the rounds, that was the question on the lips and keyboards of every journalist, commentator and two-bit blogger across the country. But the President knew they didn't really want an answer. Not the real answer. To paraphrase that actor with the crazy eyebrows, they couldn't handle his truth.

The President knew things that would send those correspondents cackling from the pressroom to collapse, fetal, in alcoves and closets and coatrooms, feverishly praying to whatever long-dead deity they currently entrusted their souls to.

And that was before the army lost control of Project Brundle.

*

On the monitor, one of the creatures flew close enough to the camera that he could make out four wings, a segmented and plated insect body, eight, maybe ten legs, each barbed along its length, ending in a jagged curl of sharpened bone.

The floor itself was a tangle of writhing tentacles lined with ragged, serrated suckers. Skittering across these were insects of a sort: shiny, faceted black legs supporting a fanged mouth inside a fanged mouth.

Farther back in the cavern a shadow slithered past. Its shape suggested a height of at least fifteen feet, with appendages surpassing even that. In an instant, it crabbed up the wall and disappeared into the darkness above.

Something slammed into the camera. The President caught a blur of fangs and scales before the signal died and the screen went black.

As far as the President knew, the creatures were still trapped inside the mountain, unable to make it past the blast doors.

Stalemate.

☛

The President had authorized Project Brundle three months after taking the Oath of Office, when the Middle East was threatening to explode for the fourth time in the past twenty years.

It was during the third Gulf war, the one in which he'd made his name, that he'd first had the idea. He'd led his unit high into the mountains of Afghanistan, on the trail of whatever bearded thug sat atop that week's Most Wanted list. They knew where the enemy was hiding, but reaching them proved more difficult than expected. Three months later, he returned to base, alone, the men under his command all KIA. When he staggered into camp, the target's head wrapped in a bloody tunic tied to his belt, someone captured the moment and posted it on YouTube. The video went viral, much to the embarrassment of those in charge of the war's PR efforts.

But then a funny thing happened: the American people weren't shocked or outraged at the acts he had committed in their name. In fact, America embraced him, and he became a folk hero to large swaths of the country. He rode that popularity to a successful political career, eventually being sworn in as the nation's Commander in Chief one bitterly cold but sunny January day three years ago.

When war threatened again, just months after he'd placed his hand on the Bible and swore to the best of his ability to preserve, protect and defend the Constitution of the United States, the President green-lit Project Brundle. Today, not only was the experiment an unmitigated failure, it was also completely FUBAR.

His advisors believed the incident could be contained to the desert, or at the very least to the West coast, but the President knew there was no putting the genie back in the bottle. Not this genie. And certainly not this bottle. So plans were already being made to protect everything east of the Continental Divide, even if it meant shredding the very Constitution he'd sworn to uphold on that bright, cold January day, so help him God.

☛

The President replayed the last bit of footage from Brundle's second floor cafeteria: it was a massacre. Blood and viscera sprayed across the walls, bones jutting at impossible angles through punctured flesh, skin flayed and stretched and ripped and shredded.

A severed, worm-filled arm twitched and spasmed across a table, landing atop a lunch tray piled with mashed potatoes and congealed gravy. The worms—eyeless white parasites from the other side, nothing but razor teeth—gorged themselves on the remains of Brundle's staff. The worms were the last living things left in the cafeteria; the first wave of invaders had continued upward, gathering at the blast doors marking the mountain entrance. Now, two twenty-ton low-carbon steel doors were all that stood between mankind and the nightmare the President had inadvertently given life.

He switched the monitor feed to a live shot of the National Mall. Tourists milled about, taking photographs, pointing out landmarks, oblivious to the slaughter taking place in their name beneath the California desert sand. The President closed his eyes for a moment; in his mind, the Mall became a field of corpses, cadavers masquerading as citizens, puppets who didn't know their strings had been cut.

But the President knew. He was the one who'd cut them.

☛

Teleportation: the ability to move things—troops, weapons, supplies—to anywhere on Earth, as soon as they were needed. That was the basic idea he'd had high above the clouds in the mountains of Afghanistan.

When he pitched the idea to his military scientists, they didn't chuckle or laugh or even smile. Instead, they asked for a few months to explore the idea; he gave them a week. When they returned, they said the idea, while theoretically possible, was not feasible under current battlefield conditions, as teleportation required two transmission pods. They did have an alternative, however: dimensional gateways. Unlike teleportation, dimensional gateways were simply a temporary bridge between two distinct points in space.

The President didn't care how they did it. Project Brundle, if successful, would be the ultimate in just-in-time delivery. A technician would punch in the coordinates from the safety of a base somewhere in the States, push a button and a gateway would open to another point on Earth. Once the gateway was established, you could send your soldiers directly to the battlefield, even if that battlefield happened to be a high mountain cave on the other side of the world. A single assassin or an entire platoon could be moved in an instant, depending on the size of the gateway, with no battleships, Humvees or Blackhawks required. When the troops needed food, you'd open a gateway and send it. When someone was injured, the medic would radio the coordinates, someone on base would open a gateway, and the injured soldier would be transported directly to the hospital. Brundle would make ICBMs obsolete. Instead of firing a missile, you'd simply open a gateway, push a warhead through and close the bridge before the bomb detonated.

Easy peasy lemon squeezy.

They'd save enough money on fuel prices alone to end homelessness and poverty across the nation. Maybe even around the world. If the world cooperated, of course.

Not that it mattered much now.

Because something had gone wrong. They'd opened a gateway, but they weren't prepared for what was waiting on the other side.

Now, everyone working on the project was dead.

Or worse. And there was no one left who could stop it.

The advisors who watched the incident footage, and the aftermath, couldn't comprehend what they were looking at. But the President knew. They'd knocked on the door. And Hell had answered.

☛

He picked up the file on Project Brundle and flipped to the facility map. Nobody in the civilian world knew about the project; very few in the military knew about it. "Officially" the base had closed in the 1960s.

A lone fortified guard shack sat at the beginning of a gravel road that ran straight through ten miles of scrub brush and lizard shit. Electrified fencing, topped with triple ringlets of concertina wire, lined both sides of the entrance road, as well as the entirety of the base. Every twenty yards a sign warned intruders they would be shot on sight. Every fifty yards a camera fed into the outer guard shack and a second guard's post located inside the base of the mountain.

The President set the report aside and turned back to the monitor. He knew what happened next. He'd watched the video so many times now he could tell you the number of freckles on the guard's face.

An alarm went off. The guard called on the walkie to his counterpart inside the mountain. No answer. He walked out of his station, which was supposed to have locked down the instant the alarm sounded. He saw smoke rising in the distance; overhead, lightning flashed, impossibly large jagged arcing bolts striking the mountain and the ground around the blast doors. The scene was brighter than the noonday sun and darker than any nightmare. From the guard's point of view, it had to be Armageddon.

The base gates finally started closing, as they were programmed to do. And the guard ran.

The President didn't blame the guard. The accident wasn't his fault. In fact, the President had been assured—repeatedly—that such a mishap was impossible. A supposedly impossible accident in a lab designed with supposedly foolproof safeguards, redundancy after redundancy after redundancy built into the system.

Whatever.

The guard would never believe it, but he was one of the lucky ones.

☛

A call from the War Room cemented the President's resolve: fifteen minutes ago, a scout team patrolling the base perimeter had failed to check in. A second team arrived and reported a massacre before their communications went dead, too.

The President knew what he had to do.

☛

He watched the mushroom cloud spreading across the California desert on a feed from a spy satellite orbiting high above the Earth.

The decision to order a nuclear strike on American soil wasn't nearly as difficult as he'd expected. The attack would be easy to blame on terrorists. After all, if they weren't at war, the President never would have authorized Project Brundle in the first place, so technically it wasn't even a lie. And he was sparing the people, his people, the truth. Because he knew now that there were things worse than terrorists.

There were tentacles.

And claws.

And teeth.

And so, the President took to the airwaves that night, delivering a speech for the history books—if anyone survived to write them, of course. He spoke for over ninety minutes without pause, giving the country the courage it needed to face another day. Despite the radioactive cloud spreading across the desert, the sun would rise again, and America would be strong. The evildoers would be hunted to the ends of the Earth, and beyond, if that's what it took.

His words gave parents the faith they needed to tuck their children in that night, promising them there were no monsters waiting under the bed, no bogeymen hiding in the closet. Repeating the words first delivered by a man much greater than himself, the President reassured his fellow citizens that despite the horrific events of the day, they still had nothing to fear but fear itself.

But the President knew better.

☞

The Next Thing

David Afsharirad

I woke up to find a man in my kitchen, standing over the sink, eating a sandwich. He didn't notice me at first, just went on chowing down, taking big, greedy bites. I was in my sleep attire—boxer shorts, undershirt, athletic socks—my hair sticking up at all angles like it does when I've had a rough night.

I'd had a lot of rough nights recently.

The man must have caught me out of the corner of his eye. That or maybe I made some noise. They say that you can feel people looking at you—some trick of evolution left over from our days as prey animals. Maybe so. Whatever the reason, he turned and saw me.

"Jesus," he said. "Sorry." He put down the sandwich. "It's not supposed to happen like this." He wiped his hand on his pant leg and extended it.

Social reflexes: I shook.

"Pleasure to know you," he said. "Why don't you get dressed and we'll talk in the living room. I can wait." He disappeared around the corner.

I followed him, shaken out of my early morning hungover stupor.

"Now wait a second," I said. I followed him into the living room. He sat on the sofa, paging through a coffee table book of Goya etchings that Jennifer had given me for my thirty-second birthday. The last gift I'd ever get from her.

"Just who the hell—?"

"Calm down, Kevin," the man said, his voice calm but firm. It struck me that I hadn't told him who I was. "Let's do this in a second, huh? You don't look so hot. Shower, shave, get some decent clothes on. Then I'll answer all your questions. Deal?"

"Fuck no, there's no deal!"

He regarded me over the top of the book and I felt myself withering under his stare. After a few seconds, he sighed and shut the book, tossing it down on the sofa next to him.

"All right," he said. "I don't like to do things this way, but . . ."

"Listen," I said. "I'm calling the cops."

"Don't."

I started toward my cell phone, but my legs wouldn't move, like when they fall asleep and they're just dead weight.

"Sit," the man said.

My legs took me to the chair opposite the couch. My knees bent. I sat.

The man leaned forward on the couch, elbows on thighs, hands clasped together as if in prayer, and looked into me. His eyes were dark pools without bottom. But not unkind.

"Look, Kevin," he said. "This next part, it's not easy, okay? I mean, no one likes it. No one. Some think they will, that it'll come as a relief, an end to the suffering. They want to go on to the next thing. They think they do. You may think you do." His eyes flashed to the mantle, to the picture of me and Jennifer on our wedding day. "But they don't and you don't. It's never pleasant, and I'm sorry about that. I've found it's best to just rip off the band-aid. I've already yammered on too long as it is."

I knew what he'd say next, but my mind resisted. It felt as if I were trying to wrench my consciousness free from my body and flee.

"Kevin, I'm—"

"Death," I finished for him.

He smiled.

"Bullshit."

"You know it's not."

He was right; it wasn't pleasant. My mind reeled. I felt sick. I raged. I called him every name I knew. I said I would call the cops, said I would kick his ass for breaking in and scaring the shit out of me.

Time passed. It must have. I'd screamed myself hoarse. But the light slanting in through the blinds was the same.

"All done?" Death asked.

"Go fuck yourself."

My head collapsed against my chest. I looked down at my pale legs poking out of the thread-bare boxer shorts, the wrinkled white t-shirt, stained with who knew what. Holes in the toes of my socks. I should have listened. I should have showered, made myself presentable. This was no way to go. And anyway, it would have bought me more time.

An idea struck me.

"I look like shit," I said.

Death had picked up the Goya book and was once again leafing through it. He turned the page now. "I asked you to get dressed. This was your call."

"I wonder . . . I mean, could I?"

He pushed back the sleeve of his sweater and glanced at his watch.

"Go ahead."

I stood on shaky legs, walked down the hall to the guest bath. I hadn't been sleeping in the master, not since.

I turned the shower on, then ducked into the guest room where I'd been living the last three months. My clothes from the night before lay crumpled on the floor. I considered dressing, but didn't want to take the time or risk the noise it might make.

I slid back the drapes, unlocked the window and eased it open. I lifted the screen out and climbed into the backyard.

The grass was cold and wet, soaking through my socks as I made my way around the house. I passed the spot where our golden retriever Molly's ashes were scattered, and continued toward the gate that would lead to the front yard—which would lead to the street.

Which would lead me out of here and away from Death.

I was sure my plan wouldn't work, that he'd be on the other side waiting for me. But no. I pushed open the gate and dashed out toward the street, toward freedom. My heel hit the asphalt of Sycamore Drive—

—and I was back in the chair again.

Had I imagined the whole thing?

No. From the hallway, I could hear the splash of water in the shower. My feet were soaked and dirt-stained. I could still smell the outdoors.

Mr. Death seemed disappointed.

"That's the oldest trick there is," he said. "Outside of bargaining."

"Bargaining?"

"If you let me live I'll . . ." he ticked off the items on his fingers ". . . give you all my money, give all my money to the poor, clean up my act, help little old ladies cross the street, convert to Buddhism-Christianity-Islam, adopt a shelter dog. Et cetera."

"Does it work?" I asked.

Death cocked an eyebrow. He stood.

"I'm sorry, Kevin," he said. "I've got to go."

"Wait!" I grabbed at his sweater as he passed by. I stood up, pawing at him. "Wait. Don't go. I'm—scared."

It was true. I was terrified. But there was something else. He'd said he had to go. That implied a schedule. Maybe if I talked long enough, I'd throw his timing off. Maybe that was a way out.

"Please," I said, real tears in my eyes. "I'm not ready yet. I've got so many questions."

Death pulled away from me and I crumpled back into the chair.

"Kevin, I'm behind as it is. You had your chance to talk and you used it to try and sneak out the back. I'm sorry."

"All right," I said. I must have sounded as scared and as miserable as I felt. I'd gotten used to the feeling in the last three months, since the wreck that killed Molly and Jessica. I'd gotten used to feeling sorry for myself, had come to like it. Now I really had a reason to despair, and while it was awful it was also . . . exhilarating.

Death put his hand on my shoulder. It should have felt eerie, but it was comforting somehow.

"It's not what you think," he said. "All that malarkey about fiery pits or clouds and harp music . . ." He waved a hand dismissively. "You know what happens, Kevin? You go back to the time you were most truly yourself. You live that time over and over, but it never gets old. It's like the first time every time. Now I've got to go."

He gave my shoulder a parting squeeze and headed for the door.

I thought about what he'd said. I thought of the picnic I'd taken with Jessica the month before the accident. We'd hiked all day in the mountains, Molly rushing ahead. We'd spread our blanket on a rise overlooking a valley and eaten and made love under the trees and the blue, cloudless sky.

"When will it happen?"

He turned. What I saw on his face made my blood run cold: pity.

"When will it happen?" I repeated, trying to keep the panic from my voice. "When am I going to die? When do I move on to my happiest time?"

"I didn't say happiest, Kevin," he said. "I said the time when you were most truly yourself."

"Semantics," I said. "Anyway, I don't care. But I want to know when it's going to happen. I can't stand the waiting."

His face softened. "I'm sorry, Kevin. It already has."

"What?"

"This morning, just before you woke up. You were in such a hurry to get out that window that you didn't notice you were still lying in bed."

"No." It was all I could think to say.

Death turned to leave. I crossed the room in a flash, grabbed him by the front of his sweater, screamed into his face. "It's not fair!"

Then I was back in the chair again, the chair I'd been in for the last three months, only moving to get another beer or to take a piss or to crawl under the covers and pass out for the night. The chair where I'd wallowed in my grief. Where I'd learned to like it—learned to love the heady warmth of self-pity.

Death adjusted his sweater. "Good-bye, Kevin," he said, and let himself out.

"When do I move on?" I screamed after him.

There was no answer.

I knew the answer.

"When do I move on?" I sobbed.

↪

What Dora Saw

Charles Payseur

Dora examined the mass in front of her—macaroni and cheese according to the ship's cook—and shuddered, reached out, and touched the spoon lightly with her hand. Images coursed through her: blood was pouring from a man somewhere in Europe—France during one of the World Wars, by the feel—and he dropped soundlessly to the ground.

The gun in the man's hand was collected, put into stores. Only once was it disturbed there, taken out on a cold winter day, thrown into the trunk of a car, and driven to Raleigh to commit a murder. After that, it was dumped in among scrap metal at a military recycling yard. Parts of it became spoons, most of which seemed to have ended up on the USS Rascal, the ship that was taking them all out into the Atlantic, to their fates.

Sighing, Dora grabbed the spoon and picked up the bowl, received a faint impression that the bowl would strike someone in the head at some time in the future, and set to eating the congealed orange mass. She wondered again why she had let herself be talked into getting on a ship and sailing to the middle of the ocean.

The image of Billy Cody's body floating in the cold Missouri River came drifting back to her, and Dora shook her head, trying to displace it. It wasn't that she was running. It was just that she knew, somewhere in the back of her mind, that this was the right thing to do.

"Not a fan of mac' and cheese?" came Agent Grant Donovan's voice, youthful and amused. He wasn't what she had expected when the black sedan had stopped at the crime scene where they had found Billy's body, not what Hollywood had prepared for her when it came to the FBI. "I'm sure if you ask, he can make you a sandwich or something."

Special Agent Donovan was small, thin and wiry, his head too tall for the rest of him, with ears that stuck out like satellite dishes. He didn't wear sunglasses or a black suit, preferring instead corduroy slacks and a button-up, mint-green shirt which he wore without a tie and with the top two buttons free, revealing a smooth, bony chest underneath. He looked too young to be real, though he assured her that he was twenty-five and had the necessary training. Perhaps it was just that, at forty, Dora felt a quick distrust of anyone younger, didn't want them to be competent because it might somehow make her obsolete.

"It's fine," she lied and looked up at him. His smiling face seemed an open mockery of her age. She swallowed a gelatinous spoonful as if in proof and managed to keep the disgust from her face. "I was just...thinking."

She thought about telling him about the spoon, because if nothing else Agent Donovan did seem to believe in her abilities. Without the actual murder weapon, though, and without more to go on, she decided against it. It was possible, after all, that the crime was long since solved. It wasn't like the spoon had shown her that as a cry for justice. It was just that certain objects were charged with energy she seemed capable of reading.

"Is it about that boy?" Agent Donovan asked, and Dora felt herself tense, a sudden anger flaring. If she had been a man Dora doubted he would have asked, would have cared. But, lacking something swinging between her legs, she had to deal with Agent Grant asking her whenever she looked apprehensive if it was about Billy Cody.

"No," she said coldly and put down the bowl of macaroni, suddenly filled with the stubborn impulse to reject it, to reject anything from this mission. She wanted to tell him that she was done, that she wanted to go back to the mainland, but she knew how that would sound, knew that it would only confirm things in his mind. And, more than that, she didn't want to go. Something was pulling her on, a feeling that she was needed out there. But no, she was not upset about Billy Cody. Or she was, but not in the way he thought. "It's just that my spoon killed someone."

Agent Donovan smiled and motioned toward the door that led to the stairs up to the deck. "Well then, if you're ready, we're about set up."

Dora felt the macaroni sink a bit inside her. She hadn't expected it to be so soon. Determined, she stood and moved in the direction he had indicated, at least freed from the terrible meal.

She reached the door and took hold of the handle, paused as new images floated up to her, threatened to drown her in pictures of men rushing about, their faces panicked, the lights around them flickering. A man was trying desperately to open the door, which seemed jammed somehow. He pushed on the door, got the handle to turn, and was flung backwards, water pouring in from the opening, rising in the mess hall, rising and not stopping.

Cursing under her breath, she pulled the door in, almost expecting to see the wall of water there to greet her. Instead there was only the stairs, and she climbed, trying to ignore the visions which were coming stronger now, more often.

Usually, that meant the events were getting closer and closer to the present, a signal bouncing back from a source drawing quite near. But she couldn't be certain; psychometry wasn't exact by any means, just images and interpretation, her own hunches after having lived with it for so long. She was used to some level of ambiguity, especially with events that hadn't happened yet, where the signal could be confused.

Still, it was why Agent Donovan had approached her, why he had convinced her to travel into the middle of the Atlantic Ocean. She was used to working with law enforcement. She had learned early on how to work within their rules, offering only concrete things, locations of objects, bodies, crime scenes. She knew the dance even if it meant not always being able to stop anything. This trip was different, though. Agent Donovan wasn't just interested in the facts, he wanted to know her feelings, her impressions. He'd been asking her about them ever since they'd left port, and always with a small, excited smile, like he was eager to believe.

In some ways, Donovan's eagerness frightened her, as a tax payer if nothing else. This trip had to cost something and it seemed irresponsible for the government to ferry her out to some remote locale just to see if she got a sense off of some sunken boat.

"They just need you to tell them what happened," Agent Donovan had said, that small smile triumphantly plastered on his face. It had been his idea. His superiors had thought it was too dangerous to just haul it up, afraid that it might have undetonated explosives or something like that. It was all vague except that they wanted her to go down, lay her hands on it, and tell them what had happened, tell them if it was worth it to dredge up the past.

As they reached the deck , she saw the small craft that would be taking her down—something out of an old movie—a clear bubble and a ton of metal and piping. Sailors rushed in their direction, and Dora stepped back, hugging the railing as they passed. New images: a man clung to the metal she was touching, eyes wide. Skyscraper-high waves rose and crashed, tearing his grip lose. Someone reached for him, but he flew past her, and Dora snapped back, released the railing like it was responsible for what might happen, and walked without speaking toward the craft.

Agent Donovan was her shadow, moving behind her as if sensing her foul mood. They reached the submersible, the crowd of sailors peeling away at their approach.

"This will take you down," Donovan said, his voice still vaguely amused. "We'll pilot from here, and you'll be inside. There's only room in there for one, but we'll be in constant contact via the two-way."

Dora nodded, having heard this before but appreciating the reassurance. She had never really liked the water—the silence of it. She sometimes felt that if she passed through the wrong current she would see every death in every sea and river around the world, in graphic clarity, as if all water was linked. If she dipped her toe into the wrong puddle, it would swallow her down so deep she'd never find her way back up. But this was different; the craft would allow her to submerge without touching the water, without having to confront it.

"I get it," Dora said, "just tell me how to get in, and let's do this." She just wanted it to be over, wanted the visions to slow. She should have known better than to follow some government agent out into the ocean. And yet she could feel something pushing her forward, or pulling her, and her mind flashed back to Billy Cody, floating in the water, his face exactly as she had seen it in her vision, captured in that moment of terror as the cord around his throat tightened, tightened. Dora let herself be led up a scaffold, comforted in that moment by the silent human contact of the sailors as they helped her step.

It was always strange to her that her gift only worked with objects, not people, but she could never pick something up just from shaking someone's hand. Touching a watch perhaps, or a ring, that was different. Some of her friends wondered why she wasn't just having sex constantly, losing herself in the purely human contact as if that was possible, as if you could make love without touching the sheets, the pillows, the floor. The idea of zero gravity intrigued her, the idea that she could just float in space, touching nothing but the still air.

As the men lowered her into the cramped submersible, Dora felt the cold surface of the sides, was relieved to find they held no visions for her, no images. She settled in, tested the two-way communicator on the side of the vessel, heard Agent Donovan's voice come through clear and calm from the other side.

"You hearing me okay?" he asked, and Dora could still hear the smile.

"I hear you."

"We're just going to be running some final tests, so hang in there."

"All right." She shrugged. It was almost pleasant compared to the ship.

The bubble in front gave her the opportunity to watch the activity outside while remaining detached from it, isolated by the thick plastic and metal of the submersible. She reached around, touching everything she could, but nothing jumped out at her, nothing showed her the depravity she knew lurked in most corners of the world.

Eventually, though, Donovan's voice returned, and pulleys lifted her out over the ocean, giving her a clear view of the waves, the blue sky, and the point, incredibly far away, where they had met.

"Okay, we're going to be lowering you in a moment," Donovan said. Dora grunted her acknowledgment and waited.

The submersible jerked, and Dora put her arms out, braced herself against the sides of the vessel, watched as the water rose up to greet her. The clamp above released, and she hit the water, the waves moving quickly up and over the bubble, cutting her off from the upper world.

For a minute there was no other sound, no light but the filtered sunlight through the water, and Dora had the sinking thought that, perhaps, this had all been a setup, that the government had determined she was a security threat and was willing to simply drop her down into the ocean in a vessel she couldn't operate and sail away.

Lights illuminated the water in front of her, and Donovan's voice broke the silence. "Well, everything looks good from our end," he said. "It will take a while to get to the site though, so if you need me to start telling jokes or something, just let me know."

"I'm fine," Dora said, her eyes glued on the area outside the bubble, the small and quickly darkening bit of ocean exposed by the lights of the submersible. She could see shapes moving at the edge of her vision, where the shadows swallowed up the waters. Fish probably, though in her mind there might have been other things as well, creatures wanting to know what would be foolish enough to venture down into the depths, where the light of the sun was a distant memory.

"Really, if you need to talk…" Donovan offered. The entire trip he had been trying to get her to talk about Billy Cody, and the entire trip she had deferred, had pushed the questions away.

"No," she said evenly, not breaking her pattern. She didn't want to talk about it, didn't really want to think about it, though in the cramped confines of the vessel, the images of that day found her, forced themselves into her mind.

Billy's aunt had first reached out to her, had heard about Dora on a talk show, had sent her one of Billy's gloves, told the story of how he'd gone missing just days before.

"I mean, what's the story about this ship you're taking me to?" she asked, aware suddenly that she had never really asked, that after finding Billy's body she had accepted Agent Donovan's proposal without really caring what it entailed. But now, sinking through the inky darkness of the ocean, she had the urge to know, felt it tugging at her mind and attention like a bird pecking at a spot of blood, wondering what the taste was.

There was a pause on the other end, and then Agent Donovan spoke, and she could tell that smile had slipped, that he hadn't expected the question. "Well," he began, and Dora could feel the wind up, the pitch. "This was a top secret project from back during the later sixties, height of the Cold War stuff, you understand."

She didn't understand, not in the way he was obviously implying, but she remained silent, content to wait for him to give more.

"Anyway, the government spent a lot trying to develop a silent submarine, something that the Russians couldn't detect with any of their instruments. It worked fairly well, too, except that part of what made it undetectable also made its own sensors a bit…tricky. So it sank, and it's taken this long to figure out where it ended up."

As stories went, it sounded like something from a spy novel, hitting all the major points, cutting-edge technology, Russians, and some fatal flaw. Yet to Dora's ears, it didn't sound completely right; and something, deeper in her mind, whispered that it was a lie. She remained silent until the water outside began to resemble the darkness of space, small flecks that might have been stars shooting through the light cast by the vessel.

"You should be coming up on it soon," Agent Donovan said, and Dora inched forward, strained her neck looking down into the water. Indeed, there was a stillness ahead, a great immutable presence like a shadow of even greater darkness, and as it peeled away Dora could see that it was the ocean floor. And there, as if resting, was the strange hulk of metal that must have been Donovan's ship. And as she saw it, Dora understood that it was not a submarine.

"You're sure that's what we're looking for?" she asked, noting the design of it, like a plane but larger and sleeker—all rounded edges without a visible opening—and complex curves, with pieces on either side like wings.

"We're sure of it," Agent Donovan said back. "We've already checked it over for radiation and any sort of signal. Everything's come back negative. We just want to know what happened to it. Your vessel will pick up a piece of it and bring it inside."

Strewn about the ocean floor were small bits of debris, metal scraps that looked to have sheared away from the ship when it hit the water, though the damage didn't look like it had amounted to too much.

Dora's submersible descended further, and she watched as a little claw stretched out, picked up one of the fragments, pulled it back in and dropped it into a small box on the vessel. She heard a slight whirring as the box closed and emptied itself of water, then depressurized. After a moment, a small panel slid open and Dora could see in, where the small piece of metal, perhaps the size of her hand, sat.

Pressure to perform pressed down on her like the weight of the ocean above. It didn't always work, she knew. Sometimes there was nothing. And sometimes even the truth didn't make anything better. Billy's face flashed in her mind again, that look of terror, that cord around his neck. She hadn't seen the face of the person who did it until after, until she was holding the cord she had found in his parent's house. Only then did she see the face of the woman she had met earlier, the one who had sent her the glove: Billy's aunt, draining the life from him.

The police had told her, when they pulled the body out of the river, that the aunt had killed herself, that there was a note, that the case was closed. They had told her that it was probably guilt that had led the aunt to send Dora the glove, unraveling her crime, a sort of confession. But Dora wasn't a priest. She didn't want to be confessed to, didn't want to stay awake wondering why it had played out the way it did, whether, for all her vision, she had missed some bigger picture. She just wanted to know why.

Shaking her head, she reached out and took the piece of metal, and images poured into her. But they made no sense.

Stars, so many stars, and a sense of time like worlds dying. She saw a creature, a person, something flying that strange ship that now lay in front her on the ocean floor. Frantic. Trying to correct—to compensate. It spoke no language she had ever heard, yet she understood it. It called for help, sending coordinates, doing something with the controls, then striking the water as everything went dark. And more time, and more, and Dora knew that this was from longer ago than the Sixties.

"Well?" came Donovan's voice, and she could tell that smile was back. Before she could answer, though, a light switched on in front of her, from the ship, and a voice whispered to her as if across a great distance. She turned, saw the ancient husk coming back to life. Another light, and another, and the water around her bubbled with activity. Fish and other creatures, before unseen on the ocean floor, darted away, or lumbered as the ship came alive.

"What's going on there?" Donovan asked, frantic now, and there were noises in the background, warnings blaring. "What did you see?"

The submersible lurched, and Dora was slammed against its side. The whole ocean seemed to be boiling, and the voice in her head was growing louder, more persistent. Listening to it, Dora recognized the feeling she'd had when Agent Donovan had first approached her: the urgent, drawing force that had set her feet on a ship bound into the Atlantic. It was speaking to her more clearly now, taking answers from her mind.

Repairs were complete, stasis was finished, Dora could feel it, but it needed to know the situation above, the reception it could expect.

Dora tried to scream, tried to push the presence from her mind.

Donovan yelled at her via the two-way, but he seemed so far away.

It had needed her close, had needed her voice.

Warn them, it said, get them away.

The engine was not gentle; everything on the water above was at risk. And with its voice came visions, visions she knew were real and happening or about to happen: the USS Rascal shook in the water, swaying wildly, trying to right itself as the ocean around it raged. In the kitchen the cook fell, knocked over a stack of dishes. A bowl landed solidly on his head. On the deck, a man was pitched into a railing, the waves licking at him as if alive and hungry, trying to pull him into the water.

"Donovan," Dora said into the two-way, "you have to get out. You have to go. If we wait, we're all dead." Her voice was weak, strained. The visions wouldn't stop. She saw the ship rise, its wake a fiery explosion of force, saw the Rascal tip and break, its hull caving, sailors dropping like lobsters into the boiling waters.

"Now!" Dora screamed into the two-way and felt a tugging on the sub, felt herself rising. The voice in her mind thanked her. She was compatible. Perhaps they would meet again.

But she was rising, rising, visions all blurring together. She wanted to cry out to it, to ask it why her, why Billy Cody, why anything. It would know. But she could feel her consciousness slipping from her, water through her hands, and it was gone.

☞

Selling Daydreams:
The Life and Work of George Clayton Johnson

David Afsharirad

When accepting the Emmy for the second season of *The Twilight Zone*, Rod Serling singled out three writers whose contributions to the show were worthy of recognition. "To Charles Beaumont, Richard Matheson, and George Clayton Johnson..." Serling said, brandishing the statuette. "Come on over, fellas, and we'll carve it up like a turkey!"

Fans of *The Twilight Zone* should be familiar with Beaumont, who wrote more episodes of the series than anyone beside Serling himself. And Matheson has gained the legendary status he so richly deserves. But the third writer—George Clayton Johnson—may not be as familiar, and that's a real shame. Johnson was as good a writer as any to come out of the "California School," and better than most.

Born in Cheyenne, Wyoming, George Clayton Johnson spent the first decades of his life drifting around the United States before settling in Los Angeles, where he took various odd jobs (including co-owner of the legendary Café Frankenstein) before deciding to quit work to become a professional writer. Success came swiftly when Johnson sold the story (co-written with Jack Golden Russell) that served as the basis of the Rat Pack classic *Ocean's 11*. Buoyed by the thrill of seeing his name up on the screen, Johnson set out to make his mark. But the dream that had at first seemed within reach remained elusive, and Johnson began to wonder if *Ocean's 11* was a fluke.

It was around this time that he fell in with a group of now-legendary writers who called themselves The Green Hand, or more often, simply The Group. With Ray Bradbury as their spiritual father and centered on their energetic leader Charles Beaumont, The Group boasted Richard Matheson, John Tomerlin, Chad Oliver, and William F. Nolan as members. Harlan Ellison made the occasional appearance, and Bradbury and Serling were honorary members.

Johnson's second (and lasting) break came when Group leader Charles Beaumont suggested Johnson send his short story "All of Us are Dying" to Rod Serling. Serling was taken with the tale and adapted the work himself (as "The Four of Us are Dying") for the first season of *The Twilight Zone*. It was the beginning of a fruitful relationship. In all Johnson is responsible for eight episodes of *The Twilight Zone*, supplying the story for four episodes (one uncredited), and teleplays for an additional four. A ninth story, "Sea Change", was purchased for adaptation but never produced due to the sponsor's concern over its graphic content.

Perhaps Johnson's best known work for the series is "Kick the Can", a Bradbury-esque tale of a group of nursing home residents who recapture their youth by playing a childhood game. The episode served as one of the four segments in 1983's *Twilight Zone: The Movie*. The big screen adaptation was written by *Twilight Zone* alum and Group member Richard Matheson and directed by no less than Stephen Spielberg.

Johnson's other contributions to *Twilight Zone* were "Execution", "A Penny for Your Thoughts", "A Game of Pool", and "Eighty Years Without Slumbering." Johnson also wrote the story for the Beaumont-penned "The Prime Mover" but was not credited. But perhaps Johnson's best *Twilight Zone* offering is "Nothing in the Dark."

The episode once again owes a debt to Bradbury, and concerns an old woman who is convinced that Mr. Death is waiting to take her. Her paranoia has led her to lock herself in her crumbling tenement apartment, never going out and letting no one inside. A young Robert Redford plays a police officer whom the woman allows to recover in her bed after he is shot in the line of duty. Johnson infuses the story with dread and ever-mounting tension before the classic *Twilight Zone* payoff.

Johnson's other produced television scripts include work for *Honey West*, *The Law and Mr. Jones*, *Mr. Novak*, *Kung Fu*, *Route 66*, and *Alfred Hitchcock Presents*. His "The Man Trap" was the first aired episode of *Star Trek*, and it is from Johnson's pen (or typewriter) that the immortal phrase "He's dead, Jim!" first issued.

But though his most important work was done in television, Johnson was nevertheless a skilled writer of prose. Though he produced only one novel (or, if you prefer, half of a novel), it is an important one. In the mid-1960s, Johnson and fellow Group member William F. Nolan spent three weeks in a Howard Johnson coffee shop, hashing out the plot of the science fiction classic *Logan's Run*, a dystopian masterpiece that imagines a society free of adults. A fine work of thought-provoking SF as well as a send-up to the Golden Age of Science Fiction, *Logan's Run* remains as powerful today as when it was written. A cult classic film starring Michael York was produced in 1976, and a remake has been languishing in development hell for years.

But if *Logan's Run* is Johnson's most famous literary work, it is in his short stories that his skills as a prose stylist are brought to bear. Johnson's prose is not so much spare as it is clean, a result no doubt of his extensive work in the screenplay format, where the ability to convey an image quickly and precisely is paramount. And it is also in his short work that the breadth of Johnson's ability as a storyteller is most abundantly clear. Perhaps no other author save Ray Bradbury wrote across the spectrum of fantastic fiction with as much facility. Stories like "Sea Change", "The Hornet", and "Devlin's Dream" are white-knuckle nightmares, while "Your Three Minutes are Up", "A Bicycle like a Flame", and "Every Other War" are beautiful tributes to friends and times past.

In interviews, Johnson said that he made a living without having a job by writing down his daydreams and selling them to editors and publishers. When we as readers and viewers discover and experience his work for ourselves, we are transported to a world created by a true original. Enchanting, eerie, terrifying, and nostalgic all at once, George Clayton Johnson's work deserves to live on, in the *Twilight Zone* and in our lives.

☛

Suggested Viewing:

Nothing in the Dark, *The Twilight Zone*, 1962
Kick the Can, The Twilight Zone, 1962
A Game of Pool, The Twilight Zone, 1961
The Man Trap, *Star Trek*, 1966
The Demon God, *Kung Fu*, 1974

Suggested Reading:

Logan's Run, Dial Press, 1967.
'Your Three Minutes are Up,' Rod Serling's *The Twilight Zone Magazine*, June 1989.
'The Hornet,' *Rogue*, Sept. 1962.
'All of Us are Dying,' *Rogue*, Oct. 1961.
'The Man Who Was Slugger Malone,' *California Sorcery*, 1999.

Suggested Listening:

The Fictioneer. (Audio CD of Johnson reading some of his short stories set to music and sound effects. Also available as a digital download.)

Further Reading:

The Fictioneer by Vivien Kooper. Bear Man Media, 2013. (Biography of Johnson.)

☞

For the Best Will Breed the Best

The ramshackle cabin and the five young, filthy boys huddled behind their decrepit, ancient father almost convinced Andrew they were doing the right thing. He looked down at the notepad, its edges furred and stained by the heavy sweating of his palms. The top page had six names on it, all male. The bulk of Andrew's role as Dr. Falmouth's assistant was checking off names in the depressing census of undesirables. The list for this week alone included more than seventy people.

Several feet ahead of him stood Dr. Falmouth himself, accompanied by the county sheriff and three deputies. The old man—Asa Knight, according to the list—seemed surprised by their arrival. His body was a dichotomy of hills and valleys, from the concavity of his cheeks to the massive hump that saddled his back. This withered man seemed decades past the ability to father anything, yet he and the five boys shared the same beakish nose.

By their stench and appearance, this clan had everything to convince Andrew of the rightness of sterilization. They were clearly feebleminded, communicating in a disturbing, high-pitched whine that verbalized a primitive biological stress. Still, Andrew was awed by the obvious potency of this old man. Dr. Falmouth had called it a devious quirk of human nature that those least desirable to breed were often the most fertile—hence the need for statutory correctives. Andrew could only wonder about the boys' mother. She must be dead.

Andrew was twenty-four and a graduate student in biology at the University of Virginia. Ambition had driven him to seek an internship with the Virginia State Colony for Epileptics and the Feebleminded, and he was spending the summer as Dr. Falmouth's assistant. Falmouth was himself a top lieutenant to the institute's director, Joseph DeJarnette, which guaranteed him a leading role in enforcing the Racial Integrity Act of 1924. These were men with excellent academic and political connections, and Andrew hoped they might show an interest in taking him under their wing.

It was the third week of June, only the first month of Andrew's internship, and already he'd accompanied Dr. Falmouth on several raids into the mountains to round up undesirables. He didn't know where or how Dr. Falmouth got the names of his targets. He dictated them to Andrew as if hearing them from God.

The sheriff said, "Asa Knight, you and your family come along with us now."

The man pitched forward as if his hump had suddenly gotten heavier and cawed at them. His long, thin arms spread out, fingers clawed. The combined effect was so startling even Dr. Falmouth flinched. The children imitated their father, making a terrible racket.

"Move in."

Andrew stared at his feet, wishing he didn't have to hear the confrontation. He knew from past experience the sheriff and his men enjoyed helping Dr. Falmouth. They waded in with their clubs. Did the children even comprehend what was happening?

Suddenly Dr. Falmouth started whistling. Andrew grimaced. He remembered the sheriff clubbing a woman's head last week. She'd not been like the others. Poor, yes, but not feebleminded. She had even offered a tearful, rational plea to be kept intact. Listening to her had sowed the first seed of doubt in Andrew's mind. Dr. Falmouth, however, had not been swayed. In fact, he just whistled the same little tune while she pled for her fertility. After the sheriff had subdued and removed her, Dr. Falmouth sang the words to the tune—

And our men and our women be blest,

Not apish, repulsive, and foolish,

For the best will breed the best.

Dr. Falmouth's whistling was almost as shrill and grating as the family's awful cawing, and Andrew bit back fiercely on the urge to yell, "Shut up!" He glanced at the scene before him. The sheriff had beaten Asa Knight to the ground, targeting his hump, while the three deputies wrangled the children. They kept up their shrieking caw as if they had no other language.

Then it was over.

Andrew and Dr. Falmouth stepped aside as the father and children were dragged to the wagon that would take them away for castration. The family had fallen silent in defeat, and the quiet made the surrounding mountains ominous, as if all Nature fretted. Dr. Falmouth said, "It is not unusual to find families so feebleminded that language is beyond them, and they communicate in bleats and grunts. Can you imagine what further abominations those five boys would sire if allowed to procreate?"

Andrew was still thinking about the girl who'd argued so well on her own behalf, and the doctor's mocking whistle. When he received no answer to his question, Dr. Falmouth cleared his throat, a corrosive verbal scowl that brought Andrew to heel. He swallowed, realizing he had no idea what Dr. Falmouth had said.

"You have other ideas about the situation, perhaps?"

"No, Doctor," Andrew said.

"As a young man of fine breeding and character, it is perhaps natural for sympathy to temper your disgust when you see the likes of these creatures. But keep compassion at bay. This country will not survive unless the best breed the best."

Dr. Falmouth whistled the tune again. Some whim animated him to step toward the cabin, shaking his head. He stopped, turning an expansive gaze upon the moist, verdant, and somewhat smoky hillsides.

"It offends me," he said, his voice rising as he turned to point at the wagon where the sheriff and the deputies struggled to load the family. "How can this fertile land that gave us Washington, Jefferson, and Madison also produce the likes of that? I'd as soon sterilize the soil itself, as the Romans did to Carthage, than let such sorry affairs continue!"

Dr. Falmouth's face reddened. Sweat dampened his shirt collar.

Andrew wiped sweat from his own forehead and blinked a sting from his eyes.

One of the deputies cried out. "Get the little bastard. He bit me!"

The bastard in question ran from the wagon.

Dr. Falmouth swiped at him as he passed.

The boy, no more than six, dodged and darted into the cabin.

"Too feebleminded to even escape into the forest," the doctor said. He sounded satisfied. "Go in and get him, Andrew. Root out our little coney."

"But the deputies—"

"Mustn't let the sheriff do all the heavy lifting."

Andrew looked at his notebook. His heart was pounding. For a moment he swore he saw his own name on the paper, as if an invisible pen had added it to the list of the day's quarries. Behind him, the sheriff and the deputies started laughing. The bitten man made a threat about removing the boy's teeth as well as his privates.

"I really don't think I'm suited for this," Andrew said, his voice faltering.

Dr. Falmouth tore the notebook from Andrew's grasp. "My assistant must be suited for everything. Inferior assistants do not become superior doctors."

Andrew understood the threat. Dr. Falmouth could neuter his future with a few well-placed words. Swallowing, he squared his back and headed for the cabin. What was he afraid of? It was just a boy in there, terrified and guileless. There was more danger from the cabin collapsing on him than from anything else.

He stopped at the door and gagged at the first whiff of the stench within. His eyes watered and he backed away, coughing and turning a disgusted, pleading glance to Dr. Falmouth. The doctor crossed his arms at his chest. His pursed lips seemed ready to whistle. Andrew bowed his head to the inevitable and pushed the door open even as his stomach churned.

His eyes didn't immediately adjust to the sudden dark after leaving the strong June sunlight. The cabin seemed to be one large room with two windows, but the panes were clouded with grime. The odor was so overwhelming that Andrew didn't even think about the fact he couldn't see until he stumbled over something on the floor. Catching himself against the wall, he blinked furiously and rubbed his eyes, retching and panting in the hot, sour air.

When he could see better, his eyes and mouth both opened wide. It can't be.

The floor was covered in bodies. Some of the stink had to be coming off the corpses, though even in the room's murkiness they looked relatively fresh, hours—not days—old. He screamed for Dr. Falmouth and the sheriff. In the dark, the walls of the cabin seemed to thicken and beat down his voice. He stepped to the first window, which was much closer than the door, and slapped the single pane as he shouted for help. The thick layer of dust obscured the world.

Behind him, sharp as a pick-ax, came a shrieking caw that spun Andrew around as forcefully as a pair of strong hands. The boy stood there, a little shadow somehow darker than the rest of the gloom. His mouth was a frozen oval from which the shriek came without stopping, as if the child had an impossible wellspring of air in his lungs.

"Stay away from me!" Andrew said. He turned, and in his panic, put his hand through the glass.

Intact, the window shouldn't have kept him from hearing what was going on outside, yet as soon as it broke he was shocked to hear gun blasts and screaming. Through the broken window, he could see why.

Asa Knight and his children had escaped the wagon and were assaulting the sheriff and deputies. One boy had latched onto Dr. Falmouth's right leg and was biting him through his pants.

Andrew turned back to the room with a surge of adrenaline. With the dirty glass broken, the sunlight came through unfiltered and showed Andrew a clearer scene. He strode forward, stepping over bodies, and took the dirty waif by the shoulders. He shook him.

"What's happening? What in the hell is this?"

The boy closed his mouth, creating a new silence in the room. Outside, the gunfire had stopped, replaced by the whimpers and moans of injured men.

The boy shoved Andrew's hands away and knelt beside one of the bodies on the cabin floor. The body belonged to another youth who was probably fifteen or sixteen. In fact, there were six bodies, an elderly man and five children, exactly what they'd found when they arrived.

But if these are the bodies of Asa Knight and his children, then who are—

The boy placed his hand over the dead youth's chest and let out another chilling caw. His fingertips seeped into the skin of the chest and plunged into the heart cavity.

Andrew gaped, and a dry ticking noise came from the back of his throat, as if he were being strangled from within. There had to be an incision there. That or it's a trick. It's all a nasty trick.

The boy moved his arm as if groping blindly into a sack of prizes. Then he grinned and jerked his hand away. The dead young man's still, glistening heart came with it. Andrew screamed and then screamed again when the boy brought the heart to his mouth, his lips opening and drawing back in a smile of relish. He looked like any child savoring fresh watermelon on a summer's day.

At the soft and tender noise of teeth sinking into the heart muscle, Andrew babbled and doubled over, half-running and half-clawing his way to the door. He fell and dragged his body into the sunlight like a debased worm, then rolled onto his back, gasping and retching.

For the first time, Andrew saw the bodies of Dr. Falmouth, the sheriff and his deputies. The four remaining children had each selected a corpse and knelt over it. The old thing they'd mistaken for Asa Knight came to stand over Andrew.

"Who are you?" Andrew raised his hand to beseech mercy and compassion.

The thing took Andrew's hand and hauled him to his feet.

Andrew watched the excision of Dr. Falmouth's heart through the same seamless, incomprehensible surgery.

"Dr. Falmouth," Andrew said again, a hopeless whisper.

"He was a medicine man?" the old thing asked.

Andrew started, surprised both by the use of language itself and the particular words.

"He was a doctor. Of medicine, yes."

"What are you?"

"A student."

At this, the old thing's head craned so far back the top of his skull hit the bulge of his humped back. He bellowed a coarse, mocking laughter.

"Much has changed in our long absence."

"Please, whoever you are—"

"Once, long ago, my name was spoken by lips that trembled at the thought of my coming, just as your lips tremble now. But do you know my name?" He leaned back as if to laugh again, but this time he let loose with a long and terrible cry. Like cubs imitating their baying parent, the children joined in. Andrew heard nothing lupine in the collective sound. If anything it sounded like a murder of crows.

Andrew glanced around, determined to run. The old man—the old thing—swooped in on him and lifted him off his feet, then flew into the air. Andrew looked down, mouth gaping in horror—but not in disbelief.

"We are the Raven Mockers, the life takers, and our numbers have dwindled with the decline of old traditions. We were slow, moving to the beat of ancient pulses. Your kind brings death faster than ever we could. How can we—what is your word? Compete?"

They twirled in the air like dancers. Andrew's tears salted the ground.

"We don't multiply like the beasts of the field. It is not our way. But I have learned much from listening to these new medicine men. I have heard their tribal chant echoing in the hills and have found truth in it. The best shall breed the best."

Andrew screamed as he was dropped like a worm, toward the upturned faces of the children below. He landed in the middle of their circle.

One of the young Raven Mockers put its hand near Andrew's chest before giving a tentative glance skyward.

At that moment, Andrew understood that Dr. Falmouth's party had interrupted a father teaching his children.

And as the small hand pressed into his skin, he knew the students were only too eager to learn.

☞

Happy Sunshine Music

S.C. Hayden

"Can you tell the court the name of the record?"

"Yes."

"Well?"

"Happy Sunshine Music."

"To clarify, that was, 'Happy Sunshine Music?'"

"Yes."

A snicker from the jury box. That annoyed him. It was a murder trial after all—his murder trial. A murder trial was supposed to be serious business. Admittedly, given the circumstances, it was an ironic title, but a little decorum wasn't too much to ask, was it?

"And where did you get the record, Mr. Veeper?"

Edmund glanced at the stenographer. He knew she was typing his name, Veeper, but it didn't matter. To the world he was and always would be known as Edmund Creeper. The tabloids had seen to that.

❧

Steady Ray's Final Vinyl was a little hole in the wall underneath a burger joint on 5th and Main. It was generally unknown to the music buying public, but to old record junkies like him, it was an oasis. Edmund had been going there for years. He'd found the record in a box of old seven inch 45s.

The first thing that jumped out at him was the cover art—a black and white image of a naked woman lying on the street. She had a black slash across her eyes, and her head was twisted in a way that couldn't possibly be compatible with life. If pressed, Edmund would guess it was a leaked crime scene photo. The record looked like it dated from the 70's. Album art like that definitely wasn't typical in that decade. Even by today's standards, it was pretty grim and belied the decidedly cheery title, "Happy Sunshine Music."

Besides that record, Edmund scored some old Trojan label Upsetters and a Saturn label Sun Ra worth, to the right collector, considerably more than he'd paid. Old records weren't just a hobby—there was money to be made if you knew what you were doing. He'd once picked up a sleeveless Hendrix Axis Bold As Love mono 45 for 25 cents at a yard sale and turned it around for just shy of six hundred dollars.

As soon as he got back to his apartment, Edmund called Rigby. A fellow beat junkie, Rigby was always ready to check out some new vinyl. Rigby dropped by Edmund's sixth floor walkup later that day and predictably geeked out over Happy Sunshine Music as soon as he saw it.

"Whoa, that's a wild cover. I've never seen anything like it. And what kind of name is Happy Sunshine Music?"

"I don't know, I've never heard of it."

"Well, let's give it a whirl."

When they dropped the needle, a burst of static filled the apartment, followed by a group of children singing a cappella.

Happy happy sunshine music
Happy faces filled with joy
Everyone loves sunshine music
Every girl and every boy

The chorus repeated again and again. Edmund moved the needle along. No change. The second side was the same as the first. Creepy kids singing—screaming really—the same words over and over without pause or interruption or musical accompaniment of any kind.

"What the fuck is that all about?" Rigby said.

"Don't know, but I only paid a buck for it, so screw it."

Later, after admiring the Sun Ra score and grooving out to some early Lee Perry, they decided to give Happy Sunshine Music another listen. This time, rather than creepy kids singing, they heard the most indescribably lovely violin music.

"What the hell?"

"Well, ain't that the damnedest thing?"

The lights flickered, then went out, but Edmund and Rigby had no difficulty seeing each other. Somehow the darkness itself was luminous. The walls seemed to ooze their own light, like those UV posters Edmund had liked so much when he was younger.

Rigby laughed out loud. His laugh was full and bright and beautiful. It filled the room and bounced off the walls and ceiling and poured through the open window into the deepening dusk.

Edmund laughed too—harder than he'd ever laughed before. He laughed until his sides hurt. He laughed until he cried, then he laughed some more.

"Watch this," Rigby said, pulling his clothes off, "I'm a deer." Naked, Rigby held his fingers over his head like antlers and pranced around the room. It was easily the funniest thing Edmund had ever seen.

"I'm a hunter," Edmund said, pretending to shoot arrows from an invisible bow. In retrospect, that should have been a tip-off that things were getting strange, but at the time it just seemed like a fun thing to do.

Rigby leaped up onto Edmund's foldout bed and started bouncing.

"I am a God," Rigby shouted, "I am blinding light, and I am deafening sound. I am pain, and I am cool flowing water."

"Then I am a hunter of Gods," Edmund said. "I will unmake what has been made. I will bite the hand that feeds. I seek no order, natural or other."

Edmund pulled his own clothes off, tackled Rigby, then grabbed his horns and twisted his head. He hadn't noticed the horns before, but at some point Rigby had sprouted a fine set of antlers. Edmund wrenched harder. Rigby brayed and snorted and bucked, but Edmund held fast.

Tiny points of colored light rained and trilled around them, like a thousand fireflies falling to earth, like a million miniature stars shaken from the firmament. The lights exploded on the mattress and bled across their backs.

Watching the dancing shadows cast on the wall, Edmund saw that Rigby had transformed fully into a deer—a great bearded stag.

The foldout bed bounced beneath them and the turntable's arm skipped off of Happy Sunshine Music. When the music stopped, Edmund and Rigby were plunged into semidarkness. The half-light of the benighted city streamed in through the open window.

They were naked and covered in sweat. Rigby was no longer a stag, but they had most certainly been rutting.

The next few minutes passed in awkward silence as they dressed, and Rigby exited the apartment without looking back.

☛

"What was your relationship with Miss Bianka Popenko?"

The question seemed to come out of the ether. Edmund was aware that he'd been answering questions for more than an hour, but he couldn't remember what had been asked, or what he had answered. It was as though he'd been on autopilot.

"Excuse me?"

"Miss Bianka Popenko. What was your relationship with her?"

"She was my neighbor." Edmund's stomach churned at the mention of her name. He didn't like to think about her or about what he'd done to her. But it wasn't my fault, he told himself. Edmund was no angel. He'd stolen things, and cheated people, and lived what some might call a self-centered lifestyle, but he wasn't a killer, at least not before.

☛

Hunched over the turntable, Edmund inspected Happy Sunshine Music with a magnifying glass. He was looking for parallel grooves capable of playing hidden tracks depending on where the stylus was placed. With a great deal of trepidation, Edmund powered the turntable and placed the needle just forward of the first cut.

After the static hiss, he heard the sound of children crying—as though someone had recorded a nursery full of crying babies. The sounds sped up and slowed down intermittently, and the effect was positively nauseating.

He brought the needle ahead five grooves and dropped it again. A woman groaned in what was either pain or pleasure or both while a little girl giggled in the background. There was a sick wet smacking sound, like a bat hitting a head of cabbage over and over, and beneath that, almost imperceptibly, someone chanted in a language that sounded like German, but wasn't.

Edmund shivered.

The moaning choked off suddenly, the rhythmic smacking quickened, and the little girl started to cry.

Edmund lifted the needle. He simply couldn't listen any longer. In fact, smashing the record into a hundred pieces was looking increasingly appealing.

His thoughts were interrupted by a knock on the door. Edmund left Happy Sunshine Music spinning needleless on the turntable and went to answer.

Shifting her weight from foot to foot, his neighbor Bianka stood in the hallway looking sheepish and self-conscious.

"Hi Edmund," she said. "I'm such a goof. I was changing the curtains, and I knocked a picture off the wall. The nail came out and everything. Do you think you could help me?"

When she'd first moved into the building, Edmund had assumed she was the type of girl who ignored people like him, but he soon realized that wasn't the case at all. Bianka was lissome and lovely, but also friendly, down to earth, and approachable, and if she occasionally took advantage of his philanthropic nature and aptitude for minor home maintenance, so what?

"Of course, come on in. I'll just grab a hammer."

Edmund ushered her inside and set her up with a glass of iced tea before rummaging in his closet. In truth, he was thankful for the distraction. He really didn't want to think about Happy Sunshine Music.

"What's this?" Bianka called.

"What now?" Just as he located his claw hammer, he heard a burst of static, followed by the sound of violins.

Shit.

The lights flickered, then went out.

Bianka laughed.

At best, Edmund's memory of what transpired after that was patchy. He knew they made love. That much he remembered. Although, making love probably wasn't the best term to describe it.

Later, at some point, Bianka said that she was hungry. He remembered chasing a pig around the apartment with the hammer. He didn't know where the pig had come from, but he was determined to catch it and gut it and cook it up for her.

He remembered leaping onto the pig's back and beating it with the hammer. He remembered the pig kicking and bucking and thrashing and scratching the hardwood floor with its hooves. He remembered wrestling with the pig and slipping in its blood and he remembered the pig squealing. In fact, he would never forget that squealing for as long as he lived.

In all the commotion he'd lost track of Bianka, so he decided to eat the pig by himself. He didn't bother gutting and roasting it. He just hacked out chunks of flesh with the hammer's claw and ate them raw. It was messy, but it worked. Edmund ate until he vomited, and then he ate some more.

When the record finally stopped, he saw what he was eating. It wasn't a pig.

Shorty after that, a police officer knocked on the door. A neighbor had called about the noise.

❧

The judge was in her mid fifties and possessed the quiet, graceful bearing of someone who knows and accepts her own worth, yet does so without arrogance or hauteur. Edmund had already forgotten her name, but he liked her. He tried to catch her eye, but she was watching the prosecuting attorney place a blue rectangular plastic box on the table. He opened it. Inside the box was a small 45-rpm record player.

Edmund's throat went dry.

"Ladies and gentlemen of the jury, Edmund Veeper claims he was compelled to murder and cannibalize Miss Bianka Popenko. He does not deny the heinous charges, yet he maintains his innocence. Why? How? Well, Mr. Veeper would have us believe that the music on this record made him do it."

For the benefit of the jury, the attorney held the record in the air above his head. The record sleeve, Edmund noticed, was different. A big yellow smiley face had replaced the black and white photo of the girl lying dead in the road. The name, however, was still the same. Happy Sunshine Music.

"We listened to the record. It's nothing more than tambourines and xylophones and people laughing."

Many faces, Edmund thought.

"But in the interest of transparency," The attorney continued, "we would like to play the record for the court."

Edmund wanted to say something, but he couldn't speak.

The attorney placed Happy Sunshine Music on the turntable. When the needle dropped, a burst of static filled the air, followed by the sweet sound of violins.

Laughter erupted from the jury box. The judge looked at her gavel like she'd never seen it before. She hefted its weight, turned it from side to side, then smacked the business end into the palm of her open hand. It made a sound like raw steak hitting a cutting board.

Edmund wondered if she was naked underneath the black robe she was wearing. He was suddenly certain that she was—naked sweaty and delicious.

A court officer fingered his revolver in its braided leather holster.

The lights in the courtroom flickered, then went out.

THE END

↪

Junk On The Wall

Tracy Canfield

People ask why I quit my job as a lawyer to travel the country buying antiques for McKinney's restaurant decor. Some of those people out and out tell me they figure it's because my husband left. They're not wrong.

❧

Evry, Indiana pretty much consists of three side roads off I-29 and a 35 MPH speed limit sign. I was sitting at Evry's only stoplight, flicking my gaze between the cop car in my rear-view mirror and the St. Anthony's medal dangling from it. St. Anthony might find lost objects. He certainly doesn't keep you from being ticketed for driving while black.

I snapped my blinker on just in case–they like to cite you for "failure to signal"–but was that the right call? It committed me to turning off into Evry, and the cop might find that more suspicious than driving on through.

Turn or keep going? Which should it be, Anthony? But the medal hung unmoving. The signal for the cross street clicked from green to yellow. In the mirror, the cop's face was unreadable behind the sunglasses shielding him from the July glare. I twisted my earring on its post.

The medal took a tiny sway to the left, like a shrug. My light changed to green, and I turned with a little more confidence. The cop car slid in behind me.

The road dead-ended at a boxy store: DOWNHAM ANTIQUES. When I parked, the cop pulled over across the street. One day, I promised myself, I'll find what was stolen from me, and I will never get behind the wheel of a car ever again.

The older white couple inside were, presumably, the Downhams. Mrs. Downham was watching that antique show on TV where they tell you exactly what everything's worth. Mr. Downham was reading a Honolulu Homicide paperback.

A window fan did its best in the absence of air conditioning, which was a little rough if you wore business attire everywhere like I did.

I wasn't sure why St. Anthony had brought me to Downham Antiques, if indeed he had. As far as I knew–I'm not Catholic–he didn't specialize in what I was interested in professionally, but what I was interested in personally. Things that were lost. Things that were stolen.

The shelves were full of, well, the kind of stuff you contemplate on McKinney's wall while you're waiting for your artichoke-parmesan dip and your mango mojito: a hand-cranked coffee grinder with iron daisies set into the wheels, a telephone shaped like an elephant with the receiver resting on its howdah. Nothing I saw seemed to merit St. Anthony's attention, but I figured I might as well do my job.

I smiled at the Downhams and put an aviator helmet on the counter–white people sometimes get antsy if you're carrying unbought merchandise. By my third trip. Mr. Downham had warmed to me in his way.

"I got some, y'know, Black Americana in the back," he said, slapping his paperback down on the counter.

"I'll check that out too," I said, not very honestly. "I see you have a nice collection of ladies' vanity sets."

"I'll be right back." He hitched at his jeans and ambled out of sight.

On average, I pay seventy dollars a pound for what I buy for McKinney's. That's a fair price. McKinney's isn't looking for museum-quality investments to re-sell when the market's up; for them, something's valuable if it looks right, and worthless if it doesn't. (Corporate guidelines: Nothing too rural, nothing too ethnic, no clothes except unworn women's and babies' shoes. And the number-one rule: nothing unappetizing.) If I see something I want for myself–a medal with a hotline to St. Anthony, say–corporate doesn't care just how one-of-a-kind it is, as long as I reimburse them and those walls get filled.

I wasn't personally or professionally interested in what Mr. Downham was bringing out from the back: an Aunt Jemima toaster cover that could not have been made before 1995, some salt-and-pepper shakers shaped like raggedy kids eating watermelon, and a translucent shard of brown plastic.

"Now this one, I don't have the whole set," he said, handing me a small silhouette of a woman with bulbous lips and a knot of hair on top of her head. It was crude in more ways than one: a nipple protruded from her pendulous dug. The number 40 was molded into the plastic between her bulging belly and bulging backside.

"Zulu Lulu," I said. It was from a set of vintage swizzle sticks. Each stick showed Lulu at a different age. She was hot and bouncy at fifteen, twenty, and twenty-five– and then gravity kicked in. Forty was the end of the line. I'd just turned forty the week before.

You know, I get that these things are part of history, and sometimes history is ugly. What I don't like is the way some white folks went from "It's not offensive because it's the plain truth" to "It's not offensive because nobody thinks that way anymore" without any stops in between.

But I wanted to stay on Downham's good side, so I just smiled and nodded. If St. Anthony had led me there, Downham had something I needed. He might even put in a good word with the cop.

My pile of purchases made Mrs. Downham nervous, and she hesitated over my corporate credit card. "It'll be seven thousand three hundred eighteen dollars and seventy-two cents," she said, "if you still want it all, Carmen."

She must have read my name off the card. I wasn't worried about the credit limit. It costs $25,000 to decorate a McKinney's, and sometimes I did two a day, with hotels and plane tickets on top of that. I just wished I knew what Anthony had seen here.

Mr. Downham plucked his book off the glass counter, revealing a cardboard beach filled with tiki-themed knickknacks–made-up gods on drinking glasses, scowling at a dried seahorse paperweight and "Blue Hawaii" Elvis in a kukui nut picture frame. Not McKinney's material in any way, but one piece caught my eye. "Do you mind if I take a closer look at that hula girl?"

Mrs. Downham's suspicions had evaporated when the credit card went through, and she got the hula girl up with a pop of the suction cup.

At a casual glance, the little raised seam along the toy's side might suggest molded plastic, but it, like her body and her crude ukulele, had been carved from wood. Fairies don't like cold iron, but that's nothing compared to how much they hate plastic. Her green paper skirt didn't conceal the spring that attached her to the suction cup, or the way her body ended abruptly at the hips. The fairy artist had provided her with butt cheeks, which said Maui 1955, but she didn't show any evidence of wear. She was as good as new. That was a sign–I know that now.

"Your kids'll love this," said Mrs. Downham.

I smiled, careful not to actually say that I had a kid. It's a bad idea to lie when you're buying fairy things.

The cop was still outside, but when he spotted Downham carrying my purchases, he spat out the window and did a U-turn back up the road.

☛

I stuck the hula girl to my dashboard. The nearest place I could pull over and sit without risking police attention was Evry's drive-up ice cream stand. It was the old-fashioned kind with a long roof spread like wings on either side, and I parked at the end, far from prying eyes. I'm lactose intolerant, so when the waitress came by and clipped a tray to my rolled-down window I ordered a Diet Coke in a frosty glass mug. She brought it right away.

The hula girl didn't look valuable. The average antique dealer might see one fairy item in a lifetime and toss it straight on the clearance shelf without realizing just how strange it was. But who goes through low-end antiques by the ton? I do.

I took my iPhone out of my purse and brought up an app I wrote myself.

HAWAII, I tapped. 50's/60's. I scrolled through the results.

"Aloha 'auinalā," I read carefully.

The hula girl set her little ukulele down on the dashboard.

"Uh, are you–" I looked over the list of possibilities. "Fertility?" She bobbed from side to side–no. "Fishing? Generalized good luck?" No, no.

Back when people had royalty, fairies did too–look at all the old stories with the fairy kings and princesses. These days, people have commerce, and the fairies have their own version of that. Somewhere skew from the everyday world, they were turning out odd little doodads to slip onto shelves. We might be able to puzzle out whatever system they have set up, but we'll never understand it.

A yellow blossom from a tulip tree drifted down into my frosty mug. There was only one thing on my screen that I cared about, and I barely dared to ask.

"Navigation?"

She rocked back and forth. Yes.

"Show me," I said, and my voice was rough with emotion. "Show me the road I need to be on."

For the first time in seven years, I felt hope, and it hurt.

✒

The hula girl kept swatting at the St. Anthony medal with her ukulele. Fairy magic and Christianity don't always mix. I was afraid to pitch the medal–seven years with the saint hadn't found what I'd lost, but who knows what kind of bad luck I'd get from chucking it in the trash?

No, wait–the hula girl was dated well after the missionaries arrived in Hawaii. I took the medal down and wrapped it gently around her neck. She patted it fondly.

My GPS said the nearest McKinney's was in Kokomo, and when corporate is going through the credit card statements, they like to see you eating in-house.

I knew the menu by heart, so I just ordered the Thai chicken salad. It actually is very good, if not very Thai. A silver-plated trombone hung on the wall above me; I had bought that in Maine–no, Rhode Island.

I used to know the guy who bought antiques for House of Blues. Whenever I saw a good selection of Southern folk art or some farmer making concrete and beer-bottle sculptures to set up by the side of the road, I'd drop him an e-mail. Then he decorated a House of Blues that was built at a crossroads, and you can guess how that turned out.

The funny thing is, my husband Terrance and I had never been into antiques. We'd lived just outside the DC Beltway–I was a lawyer then, and he worked for the DoE–and on weekends we'd go to that Shakespeare theater in Staunton or to a tasting at a Virginia winery; we'd check out anything that wasn't Civil War. One particular July day, we'd planned to go hiking in the Shenandoah Valley, but it was just too hot, so we ducked into the Strasburg Emporium instead.

The Emporium was half antique shop and half flea market, a hundred little stalls in a hive of rooms as big as warehouses. None of the dealers were anywhere in sight, and we wandered past mustache cups, old Nehi bottles with the original Nehi and bubbling mold of more recent vintage, an eight thousand dollar bedroom set in flame maple–things that had been treasured and things that had been taken for granted.

Terrance picked something up from a heap of colorful fabric. "Check this out," he said with a baritone chuckle.

He'd found a gardening glove with laughing vegetables and LET-TUCE ALONE, NO DRESSING embroidered on the back. It was light green, I think. "There's only one here," he said. "It could be Michael Jackson's new look." Back then, MJ was still alive.

Was the glove green? Could it have been gray? I think of it so often, but what I always remember is Terrance in his striped cotton shirt and khakis, his shaved head and slight paunch, as solid as a sycamore and as cuddly as a teddy bear. A wonderful husband, and a wonderful dad–at least, we were hoping for a child by that time next year.

"I think Bubbles the chimp actually did the gardening," I said.

"Tag says 1970s, but I bet it's never been worn. It looks just like new." Terrance pulled it on. "It's pretty comfortable." He wiggled his fingers.

"Feels kind of weird, though." He flinched. "Oh man, I think there's something living in here."

He yanked it off, and as it turned inside-out he twisted too...and vanished.

The price tag clicked softly onto the floor.

I must have stood there for an hour, telling myself it couldn't have happened, and that meant I couldn't have seen it.

That was seven years ago, and ever since, I've been searching for the other glove.

In Gilbert, Arizona the hula girl finally pointed me to a strip mall instead of another turn-off. I'd tried to buy plane tickets, but no matter what travel site I brought up she just stared at the monitor. Maybe it was for the best. Fairy magic and the Internet don't mix. I'd heard about some fairy gold you could spend online–it crashed PayPal for thirty-six hours.

"This is the place?" I asked.

The hula girl nodded yes, still strumming along with Jake Shimabukuro on the CD player. She had no trouble keeping up, but in fairness she didn't have actual strings to finger.

I'd bought her a medal for St. Damien, the patron of Hawaii, to go with St. Anthony, and the back seat was full of empty pineapple juice cans and styrofoam McKinney's boxes coated with coconut-breaded tilapia residue. I didn't know if it helped her navigate, but I wanted her to feel at home.

I'd driven seventeen hundred miles. Seventeen hundred miles of staring at the speedometer, of watching to see if that cop would follow me across a county line, of a fairy souvenir waving her carved hands to signal lane changes or point out police cars lurking under overpasses. At the end of my journey, I reached Jumbo's Flowers, and the sign on the door said it closed in ten minutes.

I tried to take the St. Anthony medal back from the hula girl, but she grabbed on with both hands, and I didn't have time to fight her. I dashed into Jumbo's and right past the teenage clerk who greeted me. Cut flowers in vases–no. Refrigerated displays–no. Wooden racks of balloons and teddy bears–this wasn't a place that sold antiques.

"Can I help you?" said the clerk. "Because we're kinda closing up."

"I'm looking for something unique," I said. "I mean literally unique, not just unusual."

"Check out the centerpieces. Right behind you."

And it was. It was right behind me. The green glove said "HONEY-

MOON SALAD" on the back and was draped artfully across a toy watering can and a spray of silk flowers.

I didn't want to explain a $375 florist charge to corporate, so I bought it with my own card.

❧

I re-did my makeup and checked my hair. I figured that, with luck, I'd be seeing my husband for the first time in seven years, and I wanted to look good.

In the seven years I'd searched for that glove, I'd found some two dozen other fairy wares tucked away on dusty back shelves. I kept them in a sturdy, bamboo-handled, decidedly unmagical carpet bag that had very nearly ended up on the Portland McKinney's wall. The cow-shaped pitcher kept milk from spoiling–I'd had the same gallon jug in my trunk for eighteen months, in all kinds of weather. It's nice to be able to put out a saucer when you're in brownie territory.

The swing-basket toaster warded off nightmares. The rhinestone caterpillar brooch let you get a buzz without getting drunk. I propped the hula girl on top so she could see out, then laid one other item in easy reach. The knife wasn't an antique. It wasn't valuable. It wasn't magic. But it was big, and it was heavy, and it was cold iron. I'd read that elite South American commandos used hard plastic knives, which would've been perfect, but they're illegal in the States because they don't set off metal detectors.

The glove's iPhone listing was empty–I'd spent more time researching it than everything else put together, without learning a damn thing. I put down the phone and picked up the glove.

"Any directions?" I asked the hula girl, but she rocked from side to side.

I took a deep breath and pulled the glove on. My hand felt cooler rather than warmer.

Seven years earlier, nothing had happened until Terrance had taken it off.

I reached out with the gloved hand–and my fingers jammed into a hard surface. I withdrew it.

There was nothing in front of me; the dingy room was unchanged. I felt around with my ungloved right hand–no, nothing invisible either. Slowly, gingerly, I extended my left hand again and felt something flat, rough, and unyielding. I ran my gloved fingers along it in both directions for as far as I could reach without taking a step. I wanted to be able to grab that knife if I needed to.

Something grasped my wedding ring.

I jerked my gloved hand away. "Hands off!"

The unseen touch found and encircled my finger again. It wasn't tugging at the ring; it was just giving it a gentle squeeze.

"Terrance?"

I looked at the hula girl. "How do I get him out?"

She mimed. Pull off the glove.

I tucked the knife under my arm, slung the bag over my shoulder, and peeled off the glove.

The world pulled at me. I felt a wind gusting on the inside of my skin. A strange gravity plucked at my heartbeats. It was a childhood nightmare brought on by reading too many fairy tales. The room folded itself into something completely different.

The workshop sprawled for miles and reeked of spoiled milk. Gray-skinned workers with faces like burrs, toadstools, and crocus bulbs darted between oak workbenches where others of their kind squinted through jewelers' loupes at teddy bears dressed as firemen, and clocks shaped like… teddy bears dressed as firemen.

One worker was no fairy. Terrance's eyes were baggy and bloodshot, though his clothes looked like new. He clipped a tiny teddy bear to a cell phone strap and dropped it down a moldy chute.

"Terrance," I said.

He blinked at me without recognition, and I saw the chain around his ankle. He wasn't even a worker–he was a slave.

I ran to him, set down the bag, and used the knife to hack the silver chain in two. White sap oozed out where the links had broken. The stench of spoiled milk caught at my throat, and I choked back the urge to vomit.

Terrance rubbed his eyes. "Carmen? What have they done to you?"

"I'll catch you up when we're out of here," I said. "Where's the exit?"

That last was for the hula girl, not him, but when I looked down at the bag I realized there wouldn't be an answer.

The spoiled milk smell had been coming from my bag. The cow pitcher's glaze was spiderwebbed with cracks, and its head crumbled like sand. The toaster was a jumble of pitted and corroded chrome strips. The fairy items had been made to warp reality, but in this realm, there was no reality to warp. Bringing them back had destroyed them.

The hula girl was still moving. Termites squirmed in her wood and along her verdigris-stained spring. The saints' medals had fallen to one side, and I moved them gently back into place.

"I haven't seen an exit," said Terrance, "but I just got here."

Something smashed my knuckles, and the knife went flying.

Fairies crowded around us, chattering like cicadas—but they weren't all small. A nine-foot-tall creature with orange fungus shelves sticking out of its cheeks was brandishing a wooden board at me. A necktie hung down its scaly chest. It must have been in management.

I rubbed my swelling hand. We were trapped, but while the fairy could easily have taken another swing, it hadn't. The chatter was deafening. I could make out words: costs…expenses…prices…cannot just take…

"What?" I rested my hand on Terrance's big arm. "It seems to me that you owe us seven years back wages."

Room and board…owes too much…everything must be paid for.

By my reckoning, I had paid for Terrance's room and board with seven years of my own toil and suffering, trying to find him. Seven years of bad cops, seven years of dreams deferred. But apparently, that didn't count by their rules.

"I have money." I fished two quarters, a nickel, and eight pennies out of my pocket, wondering how much silver and copper was really in them.

The fairies laughed.

Not enough…not enough… They swarmed by the hundreds, staring and shaking their heads, climbing up on the workbenches to get a better look. Their breath smelled like compost.

I unsnapped my wallet and pulled out five bank-crisp twenties, but the crowd muttered disapproval. Eats so much! Breathes so much! Have to pay! Have to pay! A fern-haired female yanked the hem of my suit jacket. Legal tender, she chittered. Thousand-thousand-millions.

I looked the manager in his beetle-black eyes. "I'll pay every penny," I said, and held out the McKinney's credit card.

The fairy crowd recoiled.

The manager shuddered so hard that luminescent fungus showered down onto the floor.

No no! Not yours!

"I'm not cheating McKinney's," I said. "If corporate doesn't allow the expense, they'll just ask me to reimburse it. But that would be between me and Visa. You'd still get paid." I pushed the card at him again, and he snarled.

"Look," I said, "you can't demand payment and then refuse it. That's–"
And then I understood.

"You can't accept it, can you?" I said. "I've agreed to pay, but you can't touch it." I laughed out loud. "You can't touch it because it's plastic."

The fairies chattered incoherently, branches and tendrils bobbing.

I brandished the card like a weapon, threateningly. "But that's not my problem. I followed your rules. Now what happens when you can't do the same?"

The world peeled apart. Workbenches flew like flags.

I grabbed Terrance's hand. No matter what happened, I was not letting go.

Together, we fell through a metallic howl, the sound like sheet metal being cut. I slammed into something cold and massive. Soft fur rained down on me, and white light shone through cracks all around.

Actually, it looked like fluorescent light.

I tossed aside a heap of pink and mint-green teddy bears and stood up in an aisle of shelves filled with ceramic bears fishing for salmon.

Beside me, Terrance lumbered to his feet.

I threw my arms around him and held him as tightly as I could manage. Seven years of tears welled up in my eyes and I blinked them back. Right then, I just wanted to gaze up at my husband's smiling face. Later, there would be time for tears, time for stories. Time for us.

As we pulled apart, he kept his arm around my waist and stroked his thumb along my hairline.

"You're getting a touch of gray there, hon," he said. "Does the salon normally touch that up?" I laughed so hard I thought the moose-shaped back scratchers would come tumbling off the shelves.

An elderly white woman poked her head into the aisle and blinked at us open-mouthed. "Uh, is everything all right back there?"

"Couldn't be better," I said. "Where are we?"

"Northern Lights Collectibles."

"Which is—well—where is that?"

"Anchorage." She must have seen the look on my face, because she clarified: "Anchorage, Alaska."

"Thank you," I said. "If you'd like any teddy bears, help yourself." I turned back to Terrance. "How are you feeling, hon?"

"Thirsty," he said. "Thirsty and hungry. I don't know why."

"We'll get you fixed up," I said. "There has to be a McKinney's around here somewhere."

⮊

As Much as to Say

Thomas Millstead

Miss Henley noticed the sweater long before she noticed the dog wearing it. The sweater was a luxurious angora cable turtleneck. Beautiful material, Miss Henley thought, and it had to have been fairly expensive. For nearly forty years, she'd clerked in an apparel shop, and she prided herself on knowing a bit about fabric.

On the other hand, the dog—to her thinking—was singularly ugly.

And how unnecessary was a sweater on such a crisp, bright, golden day. It was early October, but the sun was strong and the weather unseasonably warm. Miss Henley was grateful for this. Thursdays were her day off, and it was her custom each week to come to this park bench with one of her romance novels and a bag of the exquisite sugar-coated cookies she bought at the bakery next to her shop. She would read, nibble, and watch the birds and squirrels for much of the afternoon.

She was munching on a cookie when the dog padded over to her. Portly and nearly hairless, it was a cross between a bulldog and some short-legged, bow-legged, rat-tailed breed. The dog stopped, immobile, inches from her knees. It stared unblinkingly at the sugary treat she was holding. Its eyes, she observed, were bloodshot and icy cold.

Then she heard a raspy, raucous, booming laugh. "Oh, marvelous! Looking up as much as to say: 'Hello! I'm such a good boy! Anything for me today?'"

It was the woman on the bench across from Miss Henley. She was large and moon-faced, her puffy cheeks quivering with merriment, her eyes lost in dancing folds of flesh. Miss Henley had paid scant attention to her, although she'd been casually aware that the woman was engaged in some knitting project.

"Irresistible, isn't he?" the woman chortled.

Miss Henley smiled politely and let the cookie fall from her hand. The dog surged forward and devoured it in a single slurping snap.

"And now he says: 'Thank you, ma'am! Much obliged!'" the heavy woman announced cheerfully.

Miss Henley nodded and returned to her book. But out of the corner of her eye, she watched the dog waddle away. It paced up to a slight elderly man dozing at the opposite end of the bench upon which the stout woman was sitting. He wore a shiny, threadbare gray suit and a fedora tilted over his eyes. His legs were outstretched and crossed at the ankles, his arms folded over his stomach, his breathing deep and sonorous.

The dog raised a hind leg and sent a sizzling yellow stream hissing and splashing onto the old man's black oxford shoes.

The woman set her knitting down and exploded into whooping guffaws. She pointed at Miss Henley and declared, panting with laughter, "Did you see him do that? As much as to say: 'Wake up, Mister Sleepyhead! Time to go home!'"

The man's eyes fluttered open, aroused by the stridency of her voice. Puzzled, he looked down at his shoes and socks, feeling the wetness soaking his feet.

Miss Henley was fearful of an angry scene. Instead, the small man flashed a wobbly, embarrassed grin. He darted a quick look at the dog and shrugged.

The large woman winked at Miss Henley, then hauled herself with great effort to her feet. The elderly man took his cue from her and rose as well, shaking first one leg, then the other. The dog followed along as they headed down the pathway and out of the park.

Miss Henley was mildly surprised. She hadn't realized the woman and the old man were together. But she thought no more about it until the following Thursday when the three of them re-appeared.

She'd been seated on her favorite bench for an hour. This time, the dog came immediately and expectantly to her. She threw it a cookie and commented on the attractive sweater it was wearing.

The woman reported that the sweater was alpaca with a silk lining. She'd spent a month knitting, sewing, and fashioning it. A lot of effort, but how splendid Gilberto looked in it! How proudly he strutted, showing it off!

Gilberto was named for a former beau of hers, she confided with hearty humor. "And what a dandy he was! Oh, what a tiger was my Gilberto! Know what I mean?" She winked again at Miss Henley. "Of course, that was before I met Arleigh. Before Mister Excitement here." Playfully, she nudged the elderly man in the ribs with her elbow. His thin lips jerked apart in a brief grin, and he bobbed his head, sharing the jest.

At that point, she evidently considered introductions to be in order. They were the Gossmeiers, she informed Miss Henley. "Married twelve years now. No kids. But we've got Gilberto. He's our baby!"

She gripped the dog's head between her hands and pressed her heavily rouged lips against its slobbering mouth. "Yes, yes," she crooned, raining kisses on forehead and snout. "You're our baby, sweetie! Yes, you are, lover boy! Aren't you, baby? Aren't you, lover?"

Arleigh, meanwhile, sought out the far end of the bench and lapsed almost immediately into a sound sleep.

Miss Henley felt that good manners obliged her to offer the woman a cookie. Mrs. Gossmeier accepted one enthusiastically and consumed it with a swiftness that matched Gilberto's.

A pattern developed over the next few Thursdays. In early afternoon, Mrs. Gossmeier arrived, leading Gilberto on a leash. Arleigh followed, carrying a scooper and the brown bag in which he deposited Gilberto's droppings. Miss Henley gave a cookie to the dog and shared several with each of the Gossmeiers. Mrs. Gossmeier sprawled on the bench, her plump fingers deftly working her knitting needles, chatting effusively.

Arleigh was a retired pharmacist, the woman disclosed, while she had spent many years as a manicurist. It had been a fulfilling career, she said. She enjoyed working with her hands and had a genuine knack for it. Now she no longer needed to pursue her profession, but looking after Gilberto was a full-time job in its own right. "It's kept us on our toes. But well worth it. Isn't he a darling? Look! Gazing up at me like that! So soulful! As much as to say: 'I'm still your sweet baby, mommy mine!'"

The first Thursday of November dawned cool and overcast. Miss Henley debated whether to go to the park, but it was not yet cold enough for gloves, and she loved the autumn tang in the air. When the Gossmeiers approached she saw that Gilberto now sported a cunning red wool cap and two pairs of downy soft booties as well as a checkered lambswool coat.

"Adorable today, isn't he?" Mrs. Gossmeier asked, beaming. When the first raindrops began, she was describing how she'd created this ensemble and daintily wiping sugary cookie crumbs from her mouth. Within a minute they were caught in a drenching downpour.

Mrs. Gossmeier had thought to bring an umbrella. She stooped, holding it above Gilberto's head, as they all dashed down the pathway, Miss Henley as well. The Gossmeiers lived in a high-rise just across the street from the park. As they paused under the building's canopy, Mrs. Gossmeier insisted Miss Henley come up to their apartment to wait out the shower. Soaking and bedraggled, Miss Henley could not say no.

After toweling her face and hair as best she could in the bathroom, she joined the Gossmeiers for tea. Arleigh brought out the cups and poured.

"Thank you," Miss Henley said.

He bestowed on her one of his nervous, ingratiating grins. He had not had an opportunity to dry out, having been instructed to prepare the tea immediately. His glistening bald head and his gray wispy mustache were still wet.

Mrs. Gossmeier had wrapped a blanket around Gilberto and was cuddling him, murmuring throatily to him. "Mustn't let baby take a chill. No, no! Mama's keeping you warm, lover!"

Arleigh sniffled and sneezed.

"So nice to have you here." Mrs. Gossmeier patted Miss Henley's arm. "You must stop by again."

That was the start of the regular Thursdays-at-two visits. Since the weather precluded any more leisurely afternoons in the park, Miss Henley, who had few friends, found it pleasant to spend an hour a week with the Gossmeiers. They—and Gilberto—relished the cookies she brought. And Mrs. Gossmeier repeatedly proclaimed that she appreciated the opportunity to reciprocate by having Arleigh serve tea.

During her visits Miss Henley often marveled at Mrs. Gossmeier's dexterity, at the dazzling flash of knitting needles wielded so adroitly. The goal of this current project, she learned, was a cashmere vest that would be one of several surprise Christmas presents for Gilberto.

Another of the gifts would be a gorgeous new collar. Mrs. Gossmeier whispered this, aware that Gilberto was in the room and could possibly overhear them. She then directed Arleigh to pick up the scooper and brown bag and take Gilberto out "to do his duty." Only when he was gone did she produce the collar and display it to Miss Henley.

It was of richly black imported Italian leather studded with gleaming red and green rhinestones. An attached silver-plated disk had been engraved with Gilberto's name in elegant cursive script.

"It's lovely," Miss Henley said truthfully.

Mrs. Gossmeier uttered a thunderous laugh. "Arleigh says it cost more than his last suit! He should look as good in his suit as Gilberto's going to look in this collar!"

With the advent of December, a festive holiday air permeated the

Gossmeier household. A tall and lavishly decorated Douglas fir stood by the fireplace. Ribbon-bedecked wreaths hung in every window. Carols gently played in the background.

It was the first time Miss Henley had seen Gilberto unclothed. Mrs. Gossmeier was intently trimming the short, sparse, bristly hairs of his neck and shoulders. The slender scissors in her talented hands flowed lightly, expertly over the dog's body, snipping and clipping. "Getting my lover boy handsome for Christmas," she sang out as she worked. "Santa's coming, Gilberto! And what'll he have for you?" Afterward, with a thick brush and broad strokes, she energetically groomed his mud-brown coat.

Miss Henley sipped her tea and watched. There was no opportunity to give Gilberto his accustomed treat until Mrs. Gossmeier had completed her task. So only as she was leaving did Miss Henley pitch a cookie to him. Gilberto, as ever, ate it eagerly.

Moments later he coughed. This was followed by a series of harsh gagging sounds. He tottered shakily across the room. Arleigh had placed his half-filled tea cup on the low coffee table in front of him. Gilberto went directly to the table, emitted a gurgling hack, and threw up into Arleigh's tea.

"Oh, no, sweetie!" Mrs. Gossmeier gave an alarmed yelp and rushed forward. "Don't just sit there, Arleigh! Wipe off the poor baby's face! It's all right, Gilberto, lover! Mama's here!"

The following Thursday Miss Henley was surprised to find a handsome string of pearls dangling from Gilberto's neck. "Isn't that darling?" Mrs. Gossmeier said, although her mood was strangely subdued. "It's a necklace Arleigh gave me on our tenth anniversary. I shortened it, and now it's perfect for Gilberto. I hoped it might help cheer him up."

Miss Henley as usual flung down a cookie in front of Gilberto. He peered at it momentarily and turned away.

Mrs. Gossmeier shook her head. "So sad. He's off his feed. Can't hold anything down. I've been frantic. Feeling icky and punky, aren't we, pretty boy?"

Miss Henley looked closely at Gilberto. His stubby frame had shrunk considerably. The rheumy eyes in the squashed pug face were glazed and listless.

"We've been giving him medicine," Mrs. Gossmeier went on. "That is, Arleigh has. So many bottles and pills Arleigh brought back from his days at the pharmacy, you know. So many remedies he keeps in his medicine closet. I think Gilberto ought to be seeing the vet. But Arleigh says it's probably some temporary upset." She shook her head in bewilderment. "He never had a problem with the cookies. It must be something else."

"Gastrointestinal," Arleigh piped up in his high, quavery voice. "No need for the vet."

"Only the best for our baby," Mrs. Gossmeier declared. "Whatever it takes!"

"Gastrointestinal," Arleigh repeated.

"Antacids and such?" Miss Henley inquired.

"Of course." He nodded and darted a quick, sharp glance at the listless creature sprawled on the carpet. "And such. Of course."

"Well," Miss Henley remarked, "I hope Gilberto's feeling better by Christmas."

"Yes," Arleigh said. His flaccid features twitched for an instant in what could have been a pinched grin or a pained grimace.

On the Thursday before Christmas, Miss Henley carried a gift with her, a colorfully wrapped tin of assorted cheeses. But there was little time for holiday pleasantries or for tea and conversation. The Gossmeiers were donning their heavy winter coats and preparing to leave for the vet's.

Gilberto had been taken there the night before. Mrs. Gossmeier spoke breathlessly, in near panicky gasps. Her vast chest heaved as she related how Gilberto's condition had steadily worsened, despite the medications Arleigh administered.

"I told the vet," she asserted in blaring, tremulous tones, "that money is no object! Whatever it takes to get him well! Whatever it takes, we want him home for Christmas!"

"I'm sure he will be," Miss Henley said, soothingly.

Christmas fell on the following Wednesday. So it was but one day later, at the usual two p.m., when Miss Henley rode the elevator back up to the Gossmeier's apartment, again bearing a bag chock-full of the cookies that had proven such favorites with them all. She'd spent an enjoyable Christmas day with her nephew and his family, and thoughts of Gilberto had not crossed her mind even once. But now she could not help but wonder whether the past week had seen some improvement in the state of his health. Or whether the cause of his deterioration had been discovered.

One disturbing portent struck her as soon as the door was opened. Gilberto was not waiting there to meet her with his hard, greedy eyes locked on her cookies. Nevertheless, Mrs. Gossmeier appeared in rollicking good humor. She greeted Miss Henley warmly, took her scarf and jacket, and escorted her into the parlor, prattling merrily all the while. The tea service was set up on an end-table. Miss Henley accepted a cup from Mrs. Gossmeier, thanked her, and settled herself comfortably on the sofa.

She opened the cookie bag while discreetly glancing around the room. There was no sign of Gilberto. For a moment she pondered how, as delicately as possible, to make an inquiry.

"I hope," she said at last, "there's no bad news to report."

"Not at all," Mrs. Gossmeier responded genially. She swung her head around suddenly and bellowed.

"The cookie lady's here, lover boy! Here, boy!" Mrs. Gossmeier's cheeks were flushed and her eyes hugely bright and glittering.

Arleigh emerged from the bedroom.

He was naked and walking on all fours. His scrawny, pasty white limbs moved awkwardly, his flabby pot-belly nearly scraping the carpet. His sagging rump waggled from side to side.

Fastened around his stringy neck was the sparkling, gem-sprinkled collar.

He plodded toward Miss Henley. She sucked in her breath, for now she clearly saw his face. But it was wearing Gilberto's muzzle.

Gilberto's muzzle, hand-stitched onto Arleigh. Neatly, meticulously, professionally sewn on.

He stopped at her feet. Gilberto's blunt, crumpled, snub-nosed face gaped up at her. She froze, petrified, her hands resting on the cookie in her lap.

He lowered his snout, snuffling at her shoes, whining. He sniffed loudly, incessantly, at the hem of her skirt. Then his muzzle traveled up her dress, still sniffing, until he spotted the cookie on her lap and thrust his wrinkled face forward, between her legs.

"None of that now!" Mrs. Gossmeier burst out, swept up in gales of laughter. "Get back here, my pretty boy! No more of that!"

She went to him, chuckling, and smartly smacked his bare backside. "No cookie for you today, lover! Understand?"

Wobbling unsteadily, slinking away, Arleigh retreated to a far corner, head downcast.

"Look at him!" Mrs. Gossmeier cried out, giggling uncontrollably. "Tail between his legs! As much as to say: 'I've been a bad, bad boy, haven't I?'"

⮑

To Sail the Winds of Song

Donald Jacob Uitvlugt

Her parents wept when Areina told them she wanted to become a musician.

It was the evening two days before her seventeenth birthday, the age of majority on the planet of Kanthaka's Field. It would soon be time for her to choose what role she was to play in the colony. Her parents had always thought she would follow in her mother's footsteps as a homesteader. Thus Areina's announcement came as a great shock.

"You'll never make it," said her father. He was a squat grey man in grey coveralls caked with the grey dust of the laricite mines. Silent tears washed channels down the dust on his face.

"Musicians don't marry," her mother said, her arms folded over her apron. "They don't have children." She had already endured so much. The whispers of the other homesteader wives. This one child and no more. That she was a girl had taken away some of the shame. But now…a musician? Never.

"My mind is made up. I'm going to Sujata City tomorrow to submit my application to the conservatory there."

"I'll forbid you to leave the house," said her mother. And she did.

"I'll revoke your permissions for the rover," said her father. And he did.

Areina cried herself to sleep that night, feeling like a little girl again. Outside their habitat, the nightly winds that circled Kanthaka's Field whistled, blew, howled. And above the wind, she could hear the musicians begin their nightly concert. The trills of flutes, the rolls of drums, the flourishes of horns. The swells and diminuendos, the rhythms and tones of the song, now harmonizing with the sounds of the world, now running counterpoint. It broke Areina's heart to hear it, knowing her parents would never let her join the song herself.

No. That could not be. Areina slipped from her bed, down the hall, past the kitchen where her parents still sat, arguing over her words. The front door was locked, her access codes no longer valid. Areina took a p-suit and breather from the entryway. The front door was not the only way out of the habitat. She headed for the greenhouse, pausing only to put on the p-suit.

Even with the p-suit wrapping in her body heat, Areina felt cold. As her hand traced the walls of the greenhouse, her mind traced memories of time spent here with her mother. Planting seeds, watering them, feeding them with composted garbage, watching them sprout, blossom, bear fruit. Harvesting the fruit, while reserving seeds to start the cycle again.

Over and over and over again. Round and round in the same orbit forever. Sucking into the gravity well of this one, insignificant habitat when there was a whole world out there. The symphony outside crescendoed. Areina slipped the knife from the leg of her p-suit and slashed an opening in the greenhouse wall.

Decompression alarms sounded as Areina forced her way through the hole in the plastic wall. Her parents would come after her, but it would take them time to suit up and start the rover. Plenty of time for Areina to find cover and let their search go past her. And it did. Areina let the strains of the musicians washed over her. She dozed, dreaming of joining her music with theirs.

The sun was an hour above the horizon when she woke. She brushed dust from her as she rose, checked the fit of the breather in her nostrils, looking all the while for signs of her parents. She was alone.

Had they gone back to the habitat? Or perhaps to Sujata City, thinking to head her off? Areina turned toward the rising sun, the direction of Bo Station. There was a conservatory there too, though not as well known as the one in the capital. It was farther away, and it was not likely her parents would think of it. Areina began to walk.

Her steps fell into the jogging, jumping rhythm of the surface of Kanthaka's Field. She hummed as she walked, straining to hear the music in the terrain she covered and to add her own small contribution to it. Why didn't her parents understand? Her father took, took, took, like all the miners. Her mother was little better. In her small habitat she was trying to make over Kanthaka's Field into the image of the mythic Manhome.

But the musicians, the musicians were true Kanthakani. They did not want to change the planet. They wanted the planet to change them. To life up their art to a level no one had ever reached before. In so doing, they never took. They gave. They gave their song freely to anyone with ears to listen. They gave back to Kanthaka's Field. Gave it spirit, gave it a soul.

The moderate gravity let Areina make quick time over the rough terrain between her family's habitat and Bo Station. She paused only to drink from the p-suit's reserves of water and to down a few electrolyte pills. In spite of these advantages, the sun still set long before she saw the lights of Bo Station.

The wind rose with the darkness, until a particulate haze obscured Areina's vision. She raised the hood of the p-suit to protect her face. With the wind came the musicians' song. Areina forced herself to trudge on, resisting the temptation to listen out in the open air. She would be joining the musicians very soon. Still, it would have been nice if the dust storm had not obscured her view of the performance.

Her trek kept time with the music, and as the sun rose orange in the gritty haze, Areina at last saw the airlocks of Bo Station. She made for the closest gate, and if the guardsman thought anything of her solitary approach and her filthy p-suit, he said nothing as he cycled her through the airlock. Areina pulled back her hood and stepped out into the streets of the settlement.

It took a moment for her senses to adjust. The bright lights of the brothels and gambling dens and bars trying to woo miners to spend their company credits. The sounds of people walking and talking and eating and engaged in activities Areina could only guess at. And the smells! The ever-present laricite dust. Rancid food oil and pungent spices Areina could not identify. Strange perfumes. And over all, the rank scent of too many dirty, sweaty people in too small of a space.

She shook off her daze. She was here and there was not a moment to lose. She turned to the nearest person. "Excuse me, can you—"

The miner brushed past Areina without a look, much less an apology. She rested her hand on the arm of another passerby.

"Can you tell me the way to the conservatory?"

A dust-stained face studied Areina slowly, a gap-toothed grin splitting the grey. "What do you want with those freaks when I'm all the freak you need?"

Areina pushed away from the man as if burned, lost herself in the crowd. She let the mass of people drive her, a laricite particle in the storm, all the while searching for signs of the conservatory. She was hungry, but dared not use her credit chit. Her parents would have deactivated it by now, or could use the transaction to track her and stop her. She was tired, but dared not close her eyes. Not when she was so near her goal.

From ahead of her, music. Not the siren lures of the Bo Station establishments, but real music. At first Areina thought she was imagining things, the sound a projection of her exhaustion and desire. But it grew louder the further she walked into Bo Station, did not fade away. At times she lost it in the din, only to correct her course and find it again. And so, little by little, she came at last to the conservatory.

It was an unobtrusive place, a white doorway flanked by two images of musicians, one male, one female. A man sat in front of the door, dressed in an immaculate white p-suit. He wore his white hair close-cropped to his head. He was obviously not a musician himself. Areina's face fell.

"A recording, I'm afraid." Areina was not sure at first that the man had spoke. He did not move. "The air of Bo Station does not agree with a true musician."

"I've come... I've come a long way..." Now that she was here, the words did not come.

The man looked up at Areina, his eyes transfixing her, probing her soul. After a long pause, he nodded.

"You have the look. No doubt your parents couldn't make their habitation fee and you're looking to escape being sold as a whore."

Areina recoiled as if she had been slapped. She opened her mouth to defend herself. The man spoke before she found her tongue.

"No. That's not it. Your parents abused you, made you their slave. Made you do the most degrading chores they could think of and beat you when you balked. Beat you until you couldn't sleep at night from the pain. So you thought you'd escape to an easy life. Just run away—"

"No."

The man stopped speaking, stared at Areina again. "Why are you here?"

"I want to be a musician. My parents never beat me, and they'd never, never sell me to one of those places. Yes, I ran away, but only because they didn't understand."

"What didn't they understand? That you wanted to escape your duty as a colonist into a flight of fancy?"

"No!"

"Then why do you want to be a musician?"

Areina closed her eyes, formed her words in her mind before she spoke them. "The first time I remember hearing the musicians, I had spent a long day cleaning our habitat with my mother. I remember collapsing onto my bed, bone tired. Feeling defeated. What was the point of cleaning every corner of our habitat when the dust would get in again during the night? What was the point of humans even being here, if the dust storms were just going to scour us away?

"As I lay on my bead, listening to the wind outside, I heard something. I thought I was imagining it at first, but I realized as it continued that I was listening to a song. Someone was taking the dust storm and turning it into music."

Areina opened her eyes. They were wet with tears. "Suddenly life on Kanthaka's Field didn't seem so bad. I realized that it didn't have to be us versus the planet. Together we could make something beautiful. That's why I want to be a musician. To inspire others with the hope I've found."

The man slowly rose to his feet. He was taller than Areina had expected. He rested his hands on Areina's shoulders and smiled. "Well said, postulant. You've passed the first test. If you're not afraid of pain and hard work, you will make an excellent musician. Let me see your hand."

He guided Areina's hand to a plate on the wall, and then frowned as he read the information pulled up. "Your parents have reported you as a runaway. But you've reached your majority and have come to us of your free choice." The white door slid open. "Welcome to the conservatory."

The room was the same white as the door, more like the waiting room of a hospital than the studio Areina had expected. "Where are the instruments and the other..." She searched for the word the man had used. "... postulants?"

"Please, sit." The man motioned to a chair in front of a low counter as he seated himself behind it. "In the Kanthakani conservatories, we believe that being a musician is a commitment of one's whole self. It changes who you are on a fundamental level. We will bring out the music inside you, but the process is a painful one."

"Joy can only grow from the bed of sorrow. My mother taught me that. Whatever it takes, I am ready."

The man nodded once and raised a viewscreen from the counter. "What you are about to see is shown only to postulants. After you see it, you still may choose not to be a musician, but you must never speak of what you have seen today. Do you understand?"

"I do."

"Do you swear to keep secret what you will see?"

"I do."

A few strokes of the finger and the footage began, accompanied by more recorded music. Areina frowned as she watched, grew confused, then angry. Then comprehension dawned on her face. The video file ended and both she and the man were silent.

"You still are willing to leave your family and become a musician?"

Areina nodded, swallowed, found her voice at last. "Yes."

"Knowing that you will never know human contact again? Knowing that you will never bear children?"

"Whatever it takes."

"You are ready, then. We cannot take away all the pain, but we can make it seem like a dream."

Areina took the old man's hand. He led her into another, larger room. Clear cylinders lined the walls, each filled with a yellow fluid and bearing a musician in various states of preparation. One thing united them. Their mouths were all opened in silent screams.

Areina shivered as the man helped her undress and strapped her down to a silver table. He filled a syringe with a clear yellow liquid. "You will not be completely asleep, but you will dream. And when you awake, you will be a musician."

He injected the fluid into Areina's arm. It burned going in, and she could feel its warmth spread throughout her system. The man spoke further, but his words became indistinct, fuzzy. He could have been speaking to someone she couldn't see. Her eyelids grew heavy and finally closed. And she dreamed.

She dreamed the musicians came down from the skies like angels from the ancient heavens. They lay her down on the rocky surface of Kanthaka's Field and began to play. And their music grew stronger and stronger, more and more beautiful, but with a beauty that cut into Areina, flayed her skin from her body, pulled her apart. She screamed in pain but could not be heard over the song.

She felt hands on her body, and every touch was another bolt of pain. Somehow she knew the hands intended to comfort, not to hurt. The song changed as the hands touched her. The songs and the hands worked together, became one, changing her. Changing her with the song. Changing her into the song.

The song-hands replaced her bones with flutes and clarinets, fingers of piccolos, legs of bassoons. With burning, healing pain, they uncoiled her entrails and replaced them with coiling tubes of brass. Her nerves and blood vessels became strings, an entire orchestra of strings. Her ribs became the bars of a xylophone, and in place of her heart they put a drum, no larger than a hand. The pain of the last replacement made her pass out.

When Areina awoke, she was outside. No breather, no p-suit. The setting sun painted the dust-laden skies with broad strokes of oranges and reds and violets. At first she thought she was still dreaming. Then she looked down at her body.

She had been transformed. Her limbs elongated and lightened, as if her bones were hollow. Her skin stretched tight as a drum, with a great fold connecting her arms to her legs. Large pores perforated her body. She opened her mouth to comment on her appearance. A shrill piping came out.

With the setting of the sun came the dust storms. Wind blew all about Areina, though the dust no longer stung her skin. She felt the storm push at her, and on instinct, she lifted her arms to the sky. The winds blew against the folds of skin and carried her aloft, into the storm.

As the storm raged, it played trills of flutes across the holes in her skin, beat a tattoo of drums against her body, raised a flourish of horns. Areina swooped and swerved, dove and rose in the storm, and as she changed her body, the song changed. She and the song were one, and her heart rejoiced.

The song grew louder, and Areina was no longer alone. She had joined the choir of musicians. Of transformed beings like herself, engaged in the nightly transformation of the soul of Kanthaka's Field. With a song of joy and delight, the musicians flew deeper into the storm.

↪

Persephone

Alice Black

"Try it. You'll like it."

Jeb holds out his hand. Instead of the usual baggie, he's holding a little glass vial that fits in his palm. Inside are six ruby red seeds that glisten in the dim light of my room.

I'm looking for something special. Better than coke (been there), weed (so done that), and acid (still having flashbacks). Jeb told me that he'd have something out of this world for me in time for my party. Mom and Dad are wintering in St. Kitt's, and to celebrate I'm hosting the party of a fucking lifetime. I need some seriously strong and crazy shit if I want to be remembered. Stacy had glass-quality meth at her party, and I will not be outdone by that freckle-nosed bitch.

"Pomegranate seeds?" I ask, looking at him. "You're trying to sell me pomegranate seeds? Fuck you, man. Come back when you have something legit."

"It's not my fault you're too lame to know about it. It's called Seed. This juice is so strong, you'll trip for days. After you have one of these, you won't want anything else."

I'm not sold yet, and Jeb can read me well enough to tell when I need convincing. We're not friends: we just go to school together, hang out, fuck, and get high. His dad is some football player. New money, y'know? But he's got access to the best shit. Usually, anyway.

He opens the vial to let me have a closer look.

I lean in and sniff. It smells like pomegranate, but oddly musty. My nose tingles, the tip going numb, and I swear that for a moment the shadows in the room twist towards me. I blink, and the shadows go back to where they should be.

The seeds don't look like any I'm used to. Mom and I did that super food cleanse where all you eat and drink is pomegranates for three days.

I know my pomegranate seeds, and these are huge—the size of my thumb-nail, a blood red richer and darker than my nail polish.

"Have I ever steered you wrong?" Jeb asks, and I look up, arching a just-threaded eyebrow.

"Aside from the coke that turned out to be icing sugar?"

"C'mon babe, I was fourteen."

I really doubt this 'Seed' is strong enough to do shit, but hell. What's the worst that can happen? It's not like you can OD on fruit.

Of course, I'll destroy Jeb's reputation if he tries to screw me on this. If he ruins my party, I'll ruin him. Simple as that.

"All right," I say, making my decision. "Stay here. I'll get the cash." I hop off my bed, and pad down the hall to my parents' room. They always leave 'emergency' cash for me in case I need it, which is silly. Who uses cash anymore? Aside from dealers, I mean.

Crisp bills are tucked into Mom's dresser, behind her 'costume' jewelry that is gaudy as shit. Hundreds, fifties and the odd twenty in case her baby girl needs a cab or food. I pull out a handful and count through the hundreds. One, two, four...

"Two hundred dollars a pop baby," Jeb says. I hear him walking up behind me and he wraps his hands around my hips. I lean back into him, still feeling a little buzzed from the weed I smoked earlier.

"Can I get a discount?" I ask, shifting my hips from side to side.

He smiles. I slip him three hundred instead of four.

✒

"All right ladies!"

I'm laughing and stumbling, the Grey Goose in my belly sloshing around as I get everyone's attention. The party is fucking baller. The house is full of drunk and stoned hotties with not a single fugly among them... aside from Stacy. I had to invite her because her brother is a fucking fox.

Unfortunately, he's already fucking a chick in our guest room. My parent's room is off limits for guests unless I invite them there. Since Stacy's brother decided to be a slut, I've got to find someone else for the night. The night is young though, and he's not the only fox here. "Oh, and Gents, too." I'm giggling, and I run a hand through my hair. The diamond ring on my finger is borrowed from my mom's closet and it tugs and snags. I giggle again as I untangle it.

"I have a party favour!" I wave for the DJ to turn down the music, and everyone looks over. My fingers trace over my collarbone and slip down between my breasts. People hoot and whistle, and Stacy rolls her eyes and mutters 'slut'. That's when I pull out the vial of Seed. That's when the party goes silent.

"That's right, bitches," I squeal, and hold the vial up high so everyone can see. The less cool gasp while the less fortunate ask how I got it, and then there's the jealous freckled bitch who turns to Jeb.

"That has to be fake." The look on her face is priceless as Jeb slips an arm around her and laughs.

"Hell no, baby—sold it to her myself. Hundred percent genuine Seed."

"I'm feeling generous," I say. There is no way I'm going to let Stacy steal my thunder. "So if you want to try it, the bidding starts now." So what if I'm drunk and high—I sure as hell won't be sharing these for free. Daddy didn't raise a fool.

Jeb started the whispers once he left my place last night. By the time people started showing up for the party they knew all about Seed, about how unbelievable it is and how it's the newest, strongest shit out there. Rumour is that it's the most dangerous too, especially if you swallow the seed in the middle. Jeb's a born marketer, hand to god.

One of the girls (who's she again?) holds up two hundred in fifties. Someone else offers their Tiffany earrings. It goes up from there until a straight-up fox presses his omega watch into my hand.

He's way hot and definitely in his twenties. My fingers wrap around the watch as I take in those broad shoulders and the way he fills out his white shirt. Sweet momma mercy, his eyes make my stomach flip.

I've found my knight for the night.

"We have a winner!"

I smile coyly up at him and tuck his watch into the front of my dress. I slip my hand into his and hold tight as I lead him to the bedroom.

"Have you ever tried it before? I haven't yet. I can't wait though, I hear it's the best trip money can buy."

I want him to shut me up.

"Ladies first," his dark eyes melt me, and I smile. The room spins as I unstop the vial and shake out a single Seed. I place it between his lips and place the second between my teeth. I bite down into crisp flesh.

He kisses me, but I'm already far away. The juice that floods my mouth is sour and sweet all at once, pinching my cheeks and leaving behind a flood of sweet fire trails down my throat to my belly. I swallow: juice, seed, and all, so I can kiss him back. He's pressing me down to the bed, but I don't feel the mattress.

Instead, I feel cool water seep up around me. It starts at my hips and shoulders, creeping up around my waist before it engulfs me completely. I give into the sensation. Nothing I've ever tried has worked so fast before.

Above me, my Knight pushes me down, down, down. His face hardens into a beautiful mask of bone. Spiraling horns twist up from his skull. His eyes are phosphorescent: red gold in a sea of soothing grey. My heart thuds against my ribs, and the sound reverberates through the thick atmosphere.

His touch is cold as he strips off my clothes. I help. My breath escapes my lips in silver puffs.

My Knight whispers something in my ear before we plunge deeper into the Underworld. "You're my Persephone."

I throw back my head. My lips part as the thud of my heartbeat grows deafening. Breathless laughter slips from my lips as I answer him.

"Yes."

I wake up, the dull throb in my head echoing in my belly. Sunlight's streaming in through the window, but it's weak. I reach out for my Knight to start off round two, but find only silk sheets. I blink and grumble, crawling out of the empty bed and wrapping a sheet around myself before heading out to find him.

On the way by the mirror, I notice a couple drops of red, and for a moment I freeze. Is it blood? I sniff the stain, and my nose tingles. Not blood, just juice from the Seed last night.

I crack the door open, and peer around. Light hurts. The partiers have all crashed; some in the living room on couches, others on the floor. My Knight's not there.

Fuck.

Whatever.

His loss.

I pick my way over the sleeping bodies and head for the medicine cabinet in my bathroom. There's a naked couple in my bed. It takes a moment to realise its Jeb and that bitch, Stacy. I don't care...but I won't fuck him ever again. Not after he put his dick in that.

My belly throbs, and I grab a bottle of codeine to dull the pain before I stumble back to the master bath.

I just want to soak until I don't hurt anymore. Last night was fucking out of this world, but Christ, I can barely walk after whatever we did. He must have been seriously packing.

The tub is filling with hot water, and I knock back a couple of pills as I wait. I can't help but smile, thinking back to one of the few things I remember.

His Persephone. It's romantic right? I'm dressed up like a Greek goddess in my bedsheet, and I kinda remember that story from English class. This chick Persephone lives in the Underworld with her husband Hades during winter and in the real world in the summer on her own.

"It's the perfect fuckin' relationship," I sigh, slip off my sheet and ease myself into the hot water. "Only have to deal with his shit half the year." The water feels good, and it's not long before the codeine kicks in, and I slip into a dream about my antlered man. His fingers are cool and his eyes burn. If I'm his Persephone, he's my Hades.

By the time I wake up, the water is cold. Shivering, I get out and wrap one of the thick towels around me. Mom got them from Turkey or something. Expensive. Whatever. They're warm, I'm cold and apparently still tripping.

I'm not sure how long I slept but now I'm a prune, and there's something red on my stomach. I look down, thinking that he must have scratched me last night. I mean I'm pretty sure things got pretty wild. Only...it's not scratches but tiny dots of hot, red skin.

"Goddamnit." Talk about the worst hangover ever: the skin on my flat, tanned belly is now raised up in red bumps like razor burn. Bitch, please. I wax. The bumps itch like hell. I press the towel against it and my skin stings: sharp and hot. The soft towel feels like needles being shoved into my skin.

"Jesus..."

I stumble back out and find that the remaining partiers are all gone. All except Jeb, who's still snoring on my bed in his boxers. He can stay; he might know who Hades is.

I pop another codeine as I look through my personal pharmacy for hydrocortisone. Let's see: Percocet, oxycodone, Gravol...there it is. I grab the little tube and limp back over to the bed where Jeb is sleeping. I'm doubled over like my grandma, but it's the easiest way to walk without that horrible sharp stinging. The Master bedroom is too far right now, so I slump down onto my mattress. Lying back, I squeeze out some of the cream and slather it over my stomach. The ointment feels cool against my skin, and almost immediately the sting starts to fade.

Was I was allergic to something that Jeb's friend was wearing? I sit for a moment and as I try to remember if he'd been wearing cologne. I fall asleep.

I can feel that cold water seep up around me again. Hades waits with his spiraling horns that scrape the sky. This time as we fuck, I feel like something's watching. Hazy and indistinct, I catch a chorus of faces out of the corner of my eye. As I look at them, they fade into fog. It's unsettling, but my man in his bone mask doesn't seem to notice...and I don't ask him to stop. I don't want him to.

This time I wake up sprawled over my own bed, and Jeb's gone. Someone's padded bra is hanging from my lamp, and my sheets smell like gross sex: sweat, cum, and designer perfume.

The stink makes me feel sick, and I decide I need another bath. I get up, leaving the sheets behind this time. I don't want anything touching me that isn't cold water or hydrocortisone.

I squeeze out another handful of the miracle cream and look down. I scream.

Each bump has swollen up into a bee-sting with a white bull's-eye. I touch one gingerly. The pain is so sharp and cuts so deep that I double over. It's so bad I can't breathe. Pins and needles race up my arms and legs, only to cascade back down in a rush that leaves me shaking and sweating.

When I can breathe again, I dab blobs of white cortisone onto each bump, careful to let only the cream touch my skin. It still stings, and by the time I'm done my eyes are swimming with tears.

I haul myself down the hall to the master bedroom and tug the sheets from the bed once I get there. If this is an allergic reaction I don't want to risk getting any more of that shit on me. Did he have an STI? God, I hope it's just an allergic reaction. Please, please let it just be an allergy... I don't remember a condom.

The pillow-top mattress is soft against my bare back, and I lie flat. I want to curl up into a fetal position, but I can't without risking another wave of pain. Gingerly, I lift up onto an elbow and look down at my stomach.

It's starting to spread.

Ugly red and purple veins branch out from the rash, creeping up my belly to the bottom of my breasts and down the insides of my thighs. I run the tip of my finger over one of the red veins on my ribs. It's hot to the touch and I can feel something pulse under my finger. I pull it away, sure I'm going to puke.

I'm still tripping; it's a bad trip but still just a trip. It's all in my head. It has to be. Jeb had said the shit was strong.

I dry swallow another codeine. My mouth feels like it's full of cotton, and the pill sticks to the back of my throat on the way down. In a haze of opiates and verging on sleep, I wonder if I have Herpes.

I'm not sure when I start to dream. I'm not even sure if I'm asleep. I'm lying on the bed one moment and the next I'm back in Hades' arms. My belly is smooth and soft. The faces are back, and I can see them more clearly now—their hungry white eyes and gaping black mouths. This time my Knight is rough. This time it hurts.

It's dark.

At first I think I'm still dreaming. But I'm not. I wish I were: even if he hurt, it was better than the agony I'm in right now. I taste metal in my mouth, but I don't have enough saliva to spit. I want to curl up until the pain goes away, but my stomach is so swollen I don't think I can.

I'd give anything to be back under right now.

Grey light trickles in through the window. I fumble for the lamp and when I finally turn it on, the room is not any brighter.

Everything is grey. Any warmth in this room has been sucked out while I was sleeping. The soft shadows have twisted into those horrible faces with their dark mouths that hang in silent howls. They're terribly real and they're slithering along the walls towards me. I don't think I'm dreaming. I feel awake. There's no way my stomach can hurt this much if I'm asleep.

I reach for my phone. It's not there. It's not there.

I catch a glimpse of something in the mirror—a sunken chest, skeletal limbs that twist at strange angles, and an abdomen distended with malformed pregnancy.

I scream, but it clogs into a cough as something dislodges in the back of my throat. I double over, hacking up something onto the plush ivory carpet. What comes up is unreal: it literally cannot be real.

Two perfect Seeds lay on the carpet, viscerally red when everything else has faded to grey.

I whimper and crawl away from them. My arms give way under me, and I fall to the carpet, catching a glimpse of spindly legs and a bloated belly. The skin there is pithy and white. Those crimson veins have spread up to my armpits, down my legs and past the knee. I don't realise I'm touching my neck until I find heated flesh there and follow it up to my cheek.

I want to cry, but no tears prickle my eyes. My lips are parched, sticking together where they touch. They split painfully as I let out a hoarse sob.

Matchstick fingers creep over my belly, and I can feel nothing there now. The same touch earlier, (how long ago?) caused unbearable pain. A silver and crystal piercing that used to dangle from my belly button is now overgrown and embedded in the stringy white flesh.

Jeb sold me bad shit. He's poisoned me. Instead of dying and leaving a beautiful corpse, my funeral will be closed-casket. I'm hideous. This isn't a bad trip. I'm dying. I don't want to die.

My fingers catch on the belly button ring, and before I realise what I'm doing, I'm pulling it up. It tugs for a moment at dead flesh before tearing free and pulling along a strip of skin that reveals bulbous red seeds, packed tight to bursting.

Row upon row of Seeds are crammed tight into my stomach. In the grey light, they glow crimson.

I pluck one out, and it bursts between my fingers, staining them red. The seed twitches and squirms as it dies on my fingers. Starbursts explode across my eyes and I struggle to stay conscious. When the world has stopped pitching and rolling, I can see again. I choke down a breath and claw deep into the Seeds in my stomach. I pant and swallow my agony as I rip a handful of red juice and white pith from my stomach. Strings of red globules slide from my fingers to the floor.

I scream and plunge my hand back in for the rest.

This time the starbursts win.

✒

Voices. They're far away and garbled. The air feels heavy on my chest, holding me down against the floor. Each breath is exhausting.

My eyes are crusted shut. I try to open them: my right opens, my left doesn't.

The room has changed again: the lamp's light is nearly gone and shadows have crept up to cover a desiccated claw that rests on the carpet by my face. It's covered in red, nails painted crimson, and on one finger is a diamond ring.

The ring finger twitches, and I feel my face crease into a soundless sob. "There she is."

My open eye looks up, only able to see the wall in front of me. A shadow looms there, soon joined by another. My gaze slips back to the claw that was my hand and the stain on the carpet.

It's hard to focus. I want to slip back into sleep.

"Is she alive?" A familiar voice, I think. It sounds far away.

I crack open my mouth, my lips glued together. My tongue slips out to moisten them, but it sticks. I try to ask for help but I can only let out a rattling groan.

"That's fucked up," says the familiar voice. Already I can feel the Faces creeping towards me. I moan because I can't cry.

The shadows loom, and I feel footsteps through the floor. They stop just shy of me. Something heavy presses down on my shoulder and bones grind together. From far away I hear a snap, loud and dry. It takes me a moment to realise it was my collarbone.

"Jesus…"

"Looks like she tried to harvest them herself," the voice I am not familiar with says, and he crouches down.

He comes into focus. I feel dry lips split open as I try to pull my face into a smile. The red-stained claw twitches, and I reach up to caress his face.

The man is my Hades, wearing that skull mask with those beautiful spiraling horns that reach up to the sky. He will take me into his arms. He will bring me back to the Underworld where I'll be whole again.

He opens his mouth to speak. "Hand me the knife." There is a dull slash of grey, and then the pain arrives in a brilliant red that steals any breath I had left.

The shadows creep closer and closer until they swarm over me. I cannot see, cannot hear. They press me down, down, down while my Hades pulls out the squirming, twitching Seeds.

I was wrong: the Underworld is not beautiful.

☞

Peace

Arthur Bangs

In a forest, there was a small bridge made of rough-hewn bluestones worn smooth by the seasons. A bridge sat astride a stream swollen from the spring thaw; its waters were a thousand tongues of silver, shimmering in the morning light and whispering—in voices as old as time—the secrets of the forest.

Before the bridge stood a man, just past the years of youth, in the weather-stained robes of a traveling scholar. He had a bag on his hip, its strap slung over his shoulder and across his chest, and in his hands he bore a staff upon which was tied a rawhide cord threaded through a piece of black pumice. He was pale of complexion, his face clean-shaven, ascetic, and earnest.

The quaint beauty of the bridge and stream struck a chord within this traveler, as if stirring a long forgotten memory, and a part of him longed to rest for a time, to enjoy the play of the water under the lithic arch, and to see if he could recall that which he had lost. But he had far to go and would find no rest until he had reached his destination. Turning his back to the bridge, he continued on his way.

He followed a narrow path as it wandered through tender green undergrowth bejeweled with morning dew. With the flash of its tail a squirrel disappeared up a tree at his approach, and overhead songbirds celebrated the new day rising.

Making his way around a stand of oak, the traveler came upon a small wattle-and-daub cottage with a thatched roof and stone chimney. Past it he espied more houses of similar make nestled like grassy hillocks among the trees. Entering this settlement, he noticed that while most of the cottages seemed to be maintained with great care, some were in poor repair and appeared as if they had not been lived in for some time.

The traveler stopped. It suddenly occurred to him that he had not yet seen a single person. He examined the path upon which he stood: firm and well used, with the unmistakable marks of many different footprints. People had been there quite recently, perhaps that very day.

There were more signs of recent habitation as he ventured deeper into the settlement—a couple of pigs rooting about the path, the still-warm coals of a smithy's forge—yet still he saw no one.

A little further on, the traveler detected the odor of smoked pipe weed on the air. Hastening down the path, he came upon an open lawn amidst the cottages. There he found an ancient man dressed in a tunic and breeches of buckskin, sitting upon a tree stump, and smoking a pipe, the smoke enveloping him in a faint blue nimbus. He had a small, thin frame, but despite his apparent frailty, the light in his eyes spoke of a lively spirit. A walking stick leaned against the stump by his side.

"Good morning!" said the old man cheerfully between puffs.

The traveler stopped a few paces away from him. "Good morning, old man." He glanced about him. "What is this place?"

The old man scratched his scraggly beard. "Well, we just call it 'The Village', but those who pass through from time to time call it 'The Village by the Stream'." The old man looked into his pipe, knocked out the ashes, and proceeded to refill it. "You are wondering why I am the only one here."

"The thought had occurred to me," admitted the traveler.

"The village has gone downstream to pick hallowberries."

"The entire village?"

The old man tapped his chest with the pipe stem. "I am still here, am I not?" He chuckled. "I shall explain. Every year on this day the village goes to pick the first of the spring hallowberries, for on no other day do they ever taste quite so ambrosian. Some believe that it is because, on this particular day, the arc of the sun, the coolness of the morning dew, and the whisper of the spring breeze transform the berries, giving them the most sublime flavor."

"An interesting theory," said the traveler. "I can see its virtue."

"And so it may be," said the old man, "but I am of a different opinion. I believe that it is not the berries but the people of the village who have reached their perfect ripeness today. For on this day we all come out of our homes, blinking up at the warm spring sun, so unlike that distant orb of cruel winter, and we make our way to the berry trees we have tended since time beyond memory. Together we pick the berries, rolling them between our fingers and placing them carefully in our baskets. Occasionally one of us will place a berry in our mouth, biting through its cool flesh and savoring the forgotten sweetness that has been gone from this world for an entire year. And when we look to our neighbors' faces, we can see that they taste it too. Hallowberries are sacred to us, for through the first picking of the spring we realize we have survived another winter, not just each of us, but the entire village. Through the picking we reaffirm our communion."

"Then why is it that you are not with the others?"

The old man seemed flustered for a moment before answering. "Someone needs to stay behind, do they not? To keep an eye on things, to welcome passers by such as yourself? The task falls to me because I am too old to pick berries. It is my hands." He raised one, gnarled like a root. "Once they were as nimble and strong as any man's, but time has finally claimed them. They are no good for picking anymore." He waved his hand as if to dismiss the subject and start another. "But tell me, you who bear the pilgrim's staff and shriving stone: what brings you to our village?"

"I am a seeker of the truth," said the traveler, and the old man nodded, as if in affirmation. "My studies encompass both the natural and the arcane, but with a single purpose above all others: to discover the ultimate reality underlying all of existence. To that end, I am following the pilgrim trail from my birthplace of Trevagal to the ancient city of Agratha, wherein resides the most holy temple of Xenos, the One True God. There I shall ascend the nine hundred steps to the temple's summit and give devotion to Xenos, and should His Most Holy Light of Truth deem me worthy, I pray that He may impart His divine wisdom upon me in furtherance of my quest." A blush colored the man's pale countenance. "I fear I may have lost my way, for this does not look like the pilgrim trail."

The old man gave him a grandfatherly smile, then pulled a firestone from his pocket and, muttering an incantation, set it aglow – a common bit of peasant magic. Relighting his pipe and waving the stone out, he said, "You have indeed lost your way, young man. The path you stand upon departs from the pilgrim trail a good ways back."

The traveler sighed. "As I had feared. Advise me, old man: what should I do? Should I go back the way I came, or does this path rejoin the trail farther along?"

The old man scrutinized him for a moment before responding. "What do you think?"

The traveler looked around. Four paths met in the middle of the village, each disappearing amidst the cottages. He faced them one at time, and when he had returned to the first, his expression clouded. "Strange."

"What is it?" asked the old man.

The traveler rubbed his brow. "I…I cannot recall which of these paths I took to arrive here."

The old man grinned. "So you truly are lost, are you not?"

The traveler regarded the old man with suspicion. There was something about the empty village, the paths that led nowhere, and his entire conversation with the old man that unsettled him, as if—somehow—it had all happened before. "What is this place?" he demanded a second time.

The old man shrugged innocently. "A village, nothing more. Ah, but look at me! I am a poor host. Your journey has wearied you." He gestured to a nearby log. "Please, friend, sit. Rest for awhile, let us talk some more, and perhaps things will become clearer to you."

The traveler glanced uneasily about himself. "I shall not. If you will not tell me the way, I shall find it myself. Good day to you."

The old man did not respond, but merely watched him, and without another word the traveler went on his way, choosing a path based on the position of the morning sun. He followed its winding course between the buildings, turning so often that he began to doubt whether it even led out of the village, until, coming around the corner of a cottage, he found himself once more on the village green. The old man showed no surprise at his reappearance, but simply continued to smoke his pipe.

The traveler glared at him. "This village is bewitched."

The old man shook his head slowly. "I was much like you, once. So restless. So full of certainty and ignorance."

Despite his mounting apprehension, the young man in his pride could not help but be irritated by the pity on the old man's face, and he forced a scornful laugh. Perhaps by bantering with the presumptuous old fool he could discern some manner of escape from this place. "Is that so? And then what happened?"

The old man held out his hands, taking in the entire village. "This village happened. I was not born here, but in the town of Seacliff upon the Auralian coast. Do you know it?"

The traveler crossed his arms. "Yes."

The old man puffed on his pipe, a soft smile gracing his weathered face. "I was a stonecutter. Among the best in a town famed for its stonework, or so I thought myself to be. One day, when my apprenticeship with the town's master stonecutter was nearing its end, I decided to leave, to travel to far off Agratha and offer my skills in the building of the temple, which was finally nearing completion almost one thousand years after the laying of its cornerstone."

"The temple has been finished for ten years now."

"Twenty years, if the report I have heard is true. But remember: this was a long time ago, when I was still a young man, filled with visions of the glories I would achieve through stone—all in devotion to Xenos, of course. So I packed up my things and, like you, took to the pilgrim trail. And just like you I strayed from the path and found myself in this village."

The traveler snorted. "I suppose there is no point in asking you the way, if after all these years you still have not figured out how to leave."

The old man laughed. "I was not that lost, young man. Or perhaps I was, though not in the manner you mean.

"I can remember it like it was yesterday. It was a glorious spring morning much like this one. I had just crossed the old stone bridge, all but certain that I had gone the wrong way, when I came upon a young lass coming to fetch some water from the stream. She was the most exquisite creature I had ever seen: amber hair floating on the wind like a corona of liquid fire, lips so soft and pink they begged to be kissed, and eyes as blue as halcyon flowers. It must have been those eyes that named her, for she was called Flora, and like the halcyon's fragrance, she was a comfort and joy to all who knew her. The moment I saw Flora, nothing else mattered to me anymore: not the pilgrim trail, not Agratha and the temple of Xenos, not even stonecutting. Throwing myself at her feet, I pledged my undying love to her, and though she responded to this foolishness with a laugh so lovely it brought tears to my eyes, she accepted. We were married on Midsummer's Day." For a moment the traveler caught a glimmer of the young stonecutter in the ancient face as it gazed into the past, but when the old man regarded him once more it was gone. "That was seventy years ago. So you see, young man, though you may think you know both your path and destination, by becoming truly lost you may find what it is you truly need. I had been so sure of my dreams of achieving eternal glory through my craft, but in Flora and this village, I found peace, and realized I wanted nothing else."

The traveler's disdain for the old man was tempered by the telling of his tale, and by the time he had finished it, a smile had dawned upon the young man's face. "Is your wife picking berries with the others?"

The old man looked down at the grass at his feet and smoked meditatively for a few moments before responding. "She died. Ten years ago. A stranger arrived, and with him the Rotting Bane."

The traveler nodded sadly. That explained the empty cottages. "I am sorry."

The old man grimaced, then, knocking the ash from his pipe, forced a smile. "Our village was diminished, but the children who survived have grown up strong, and we now have a new generation and the cottages to house them. As for Flora and I, we had many years together, saw the birth of three children, seven grandchildren, and ten great-grandchildren. Most of them survived infancy and some survived the Rotting Bane as well. Nothing is certain in this world, young man, and the most any of us can hope for is happiness for a while. Flora and I had a lifetime's worth."

"Still," said the traveler, "it is a pity that you never had a chance to work on the great temple."

"It is true; living in this village, I had to learn the ways of the fruit picker, farmer, and hunter, and there was only the occasional need for my stonecutting skills. But there is more to life than cutting stone."

"But with Xenos guiding your hands you could have created a work of devotion to last the ages!"

The old man shook his head. "What is the worth of an eternity etched in stone? My Flora may be dead these ten years, yet still I hear the lilt of her voice on the breeze, see the flash of her eyes in the stream where I first beheld her. This village, this forest, it is full of her. So long as these things last, Flora will never truly be gone."

"No," insisted the traveler. "That is no real immortality. There is something more."

"Your 'ultimate reality?'" offered the old man.

"Exactly! All surface existence is ephemeral. You said yourself that happiness is fleeting. Your Flora is gone, and all memory of her will perish with you and all who knew her. But to discover the ultimate reality... it is to become one with the infinite! And with Xenos' grace I shall discover it."

The old man stared hard at the traveler for a long time before finally breaking his silence. "The immortality you seek is a cold, empty existence." He sighed and slowly got to his feet, leaning heavily on his walking stick. "I wish I could convince you otherwise, young man, but I can see you are anxious to continue on your way, and I am keeping you. Come: I shall show you where you need to go." Without as much as a backward glance he started down a path. The traveler followed, his lingering wariness about the village and his strange guide giving way to a sense of relief at the prospect of resuming his journey. Soon they had left the village behind them and the path once more twisted through the forest.

"I do not recall this way," said the traveler. "Does it rejoin the pilgrim trail?"

"Patience. Just a little farther."

The path ended in a clearing amidst the trees, in the middle of which rested a boulder as tall as a man. The forest floor surrounding the boulder was a cerulean mist of halcyon in full spring bloom. They came up to the old man's knees as he waded through them with great care, and the clearing was filled with their soothing aroma.

"What is this place?" asked the traveler.

"Come and see, Colin."

"Wait!" the traveler shouted, stumbling through the flowers after the old man. "I never told you my name!" He grabbed at him and somehow missed, falling to the ground.

"Yes, you did," said the old man, who had reached the boulder. "You just do not recall it. Look."

The traveler got to his feet and approached the stone. Its surface had been smoothed and words were inscribed there:

Here lie those who perished from the Rotting Bane

in the 4971st year after the Cataclysm of Fire.

May they rest in peace.

Below the epitaph was a list of names that disappeared into the flowers.

"4971," said the traveler, "but that is this year."

"No," said the old man. "The year is 4981."

The traveler shook his head but said nothing. He read the first name on the stone: Flora, wife of Astan. Continuing down the list of the dead, he had to peer through the halcyon to read the last name:

Colin of Trevagal.

"I don't …how… " he stammered.

"It was ten years ago, ten years to the day, that you arrived here, feverish and dying. It was evening, and we had just returned from the picking of the hallowberries. Even from a distance I could see upon your face the yellow cast and purple scales of the Rotting Bane. I shouted to the others to go to their houses and bar their doors, and with my family did the same. You came to our cottage first, begging for aid. Though she knew the danger, Flora wanted to let you in, to give you comfort in your final hours," the old man looked away from the traveler, "but I forbade it. 'By taking him in,' I told her, 'you would risk all of our lives. 'Let the forest take him.' Finding no welcome in the village, you continued on your way. But you did not go far: you collapsed where we now stand. All that night, hiding in our homes, we could hear your cries in the darkness, cursing us for our callousness, and Xenos for abandoning you. By dawn, the cries had ceased, and we thought we were saved. But a few days later Flora fell sick."

In a flash of memory, it all came back to the traveler. "No, no, this is not possible." Even as he uttered those words, he knew the old man spoke true, yet still he persisted. "I cannot be dead! I must reach Agratha!"

The old man nodded sadly. "So you told me nine years ago, when you appeared once more in our village, searching for the way back to the pilgrim trail. It was on that day I learned your name, and soon after I added it to the others on the stone, hoping that if I did so you might remain at peace. But no: on this day, every year for the past ten years, you have returned.

"You asked why the others are not here. Yes, today is the day for picking the first of the hallowberries, but we did not always all go at once to do the picking. Today, the others left because of you. They knew you would return. They knew you would arrive with no memory of the day you died or of any other day for the past ten years. They knew you would wander the village, and unable to leave, demand explanations from them and accuse them of witchcraft. Unable to bear your presence, the memory of what they—we—did, they will stay away until you have returned to wherever it is you go when you are not here.

"And each year I remain behind, waiting for you. First I tried to lead you back over the bridge, but before we could even reach the edge of the village, you disappeared, only to find yourself once more upon the green, before my door. It is not until I bring you here that you finally find your rest—but only for one more year. And so I try, so hard I try, to convince you to cease your wanderings, to find peace within yourself, a final peace. And each year I fail."

His strength leaving him, the traveler sank to his knees, his staff falling from his grasp and disappearing into the halcyon. "I was to do great things. I was to discover the ultimate reality... I deserved more than this!"

"Yes, you did. But it is your outrage over this injustice and your endless desire for what cannot be that keep you here, that make you and I reenact this same tragedy every year. You need to let it go."

"As you have?" murmured the traveler. He could feel the sunlight filtering through him as if through the motes that float upon the air. "You speak of having your fill of happiness, of finding peace, but is it so? Have you truly let go of your anger at the man who killed your Flora?"

The old man's eyes glistened in the morning light. "I... I have tried. But it is not just my anger that haunts me; it is my guilt as well. I curse you for having strayed from the pilgrim trail in one breath and myself for barring my door to you in the next. You may be condemned to suffer this pain once a year, but I suffer it every day. Please, Colin, for the both of us: let us end this!"

"I cannot..." whispered the traveler, fading into the halcyon and grass. "Robbed of all else, it is the only thing left to me."

The clearing was quiet, save for the innocent melodies of songbirds overhead.

The old man stood there for some time, staring at the place where the traveler had been.

"Until next year," he sighed and slowly made his way back to the village.

☞

The Night Visitor

Sylvia Greenwich

In the cool blue front parlor of Number 19 East Summer Street, Jonathan Beecham was watching television with the sound turned down, not wanting to disturb the house's only other human occupant, his mother, Eloise, who was asleep in the room down the hall from the kitchen.

The room had once been Jonathan's father's study, but Jonathan had converted it after his father's death, when Eloise had taken her "bad turn," as they called it, private family code for a certain refusal to confront the realities of life.

Jonathan's father, Martin Beecham —Marty to the men with whom he'd served in the Pacific Theater, an experience about which he never spoke except to others who'd been there—had populated his study with artifacts of his experience. Having made his way back to America by way of a rambling detour that took him across the breadth of Europe, he'd accumulated an almost alarming number of items, all of which Eloise had refused to dust.

"The room frightens me," she'd say, birdlike shoulders shuddering beneath one of the draped thin sweaters she wore in all weather.

Once, a Turkish hookah had held pride of place on the long shelves Father had built into one wall, the apparatus' snake-like hose and yellowed ivory mouthpiece suggesting movement and life, in sharp contrast to the dull, vacant stare of a human skull, picked up from some remote, unnamed island, perhaps, or maybe stolen from a neglected catacomb under a damp French city.

Jonathan had never asked. Father—always Father, the capital implied as well as intoned—rarely looked at Jonathan but rather through him, as if Jonathan were transparent, or a screen upon which were projected the images of Father's own youth, images more interesting than Jonathan's pedestrian private school adventures, his good grades, decent college career, and respectable if unremarkable office job.

Of course, the skull wasn't the only mystery Father's study offered to Jonathan.

Coming home late in the steady drizzle of a cold November night or the misty cool glow of an early spring thaw...

Coming home any time, really, after dark, when shadows cast their long, obscuring fingers over the walkway at the side of the house and the narrow hallway that ran back to Father's room...

Coming home late from a study session or a movie night with friends—back when he had friends, jovial, smiling, unserious young men and quick-to-laugh girls with bright hair and flashing teeth, friends behind whose boisterous good natures Jonathan could safely hide...

Coming home, Jonathan would hear the indistinct rumble of a strange man's voice carrying down the dark hallway from Father's study. He tried to resist his curiosity, knew that if he were caught, his father would see it as a betrayal of their implicit agreement to occupy the same spaces but never at the same time.

The guttural syllables, blurred strangely by the weight of Jonathan's intent and breathing silence, drew him inexorably through the shadows, practically on his tiptoes, foolish, ridiculous, avoiding the familiar worn places on the floor that would creak underfoot.

For all his stealth, when Jonathan reached the coveted place outside the closed door, the sounds would cease, conversation cutting off abruptly into an eerie silence that made the flesh on his arms creep and startled the hair at the nape of his neck into standing.

Resisting the cold urgency slinking through his bowels, Jonathan would escape the way he'd come, the resumed conversation driving a resentful straightness up his spine by the time he reached the kitchen doorway and heard the men once again joining in the kind of talk he was barred from sharing.

Stranger still than the preternatural silence invited by Jonathan's sneaking was the mysterious source of the discourse.

There was never an unknown car parked in front of their house, never an extra tumbler in the sink the next morning. Jonathan didn't know what to make of his father's nocturnal visitor, but he was afraid to ask, afraid of violating one of the many unspoken rules of their family, so he never did find out to whom Father spoke on those strange, dark nights, and Father went right on looking through his son.

When Father had declined into an early senility, Alzheimer's taking its toll on memory, Jonathan had been quite literally obliterated, replaced in Father's far-seeing gaze by Jeb or Stevie or Lean-to or Porkpie, any of the myriad young men with whom Father must have served. Every time Father called him by another man's name, Jonathan felt a frisson of excitement at having unwittingly pulled back the curtain to expose his father's secret past. The guilt he felt at eating up his father's revelations was matched only by his relief when Father fell silent, dozing or in a fugue: Mother couldn't stand Father's mutterings.

From his father's bedside in the study, which had become and would remain forever after a sickroom, Jonathan would hear his mother in the kitchen puttering over supper and talking, always talking to herself. Jonathan could never discern the topic of her conversation, but he recognized the tone—querulous, aggrieved, and anxious. She resented Father spending so much time in a past that did not include her.

"Does he ever speak of his Eloise?" she wondered once, just a few days before Father had gone down into the last, long sleep of forgetting.

"Of course, Mother," Jonathan had lied. "He speaks of you often."

Despite Father's rapid decline, the inevitable end seemed to have dangled indefinitely, a blade refusing to fall, and Father's increasing confusion was matched only by Mother's growing unhappiness.

"What do you need, Mother?" Jonathan would ask five, fifteen, fifty times a day, leaving his father's bedside and trailing the tightening chains of anxiety behind him as he abandoned one parent for the other. "What can I do?"

She never had an answer, only wanted the attention of his patient self, though it was an effort to share a cup of tea with her when he could make out from down the hall his father's restless, uneasy ramblings.

At night, when Mother had finally fallen into a fitful sleep in her upstairs room, Jonathan would sneak to the kitchen for a quiet cup and a few moments' peace over the evening paper. If his hands shook on the thin page as the old, unknowable voices started up from his father's sickroom, Jonathan pretended it wasn't so. On the long, lonely nights of his vigil, Jonathan would swallow the bitterness of his sorrow at knowing that even on the doorstep of death, his father preferred the company of ghosts to his living son.

He swallowed the bitterness and the sorrow another time when he said only good words over his father's body, over the shining brown box that held his father's bones, over the broken earth and the bright green sod that blanketed his final resting place.

And then he returned home to the cool blue living room in the neat white house with the black trim, and he waited for his mother's voice to also cease.

Soon enough, though she showed no physical signs of decay, Mother was installed in the downstairs sickroom which had been sanitized, of course, of all visible evidence of Father. Only the lingering odor of cherry pipe smoke—a vice of which Mother had broken Father a few years before his death—and the occasional suggestion of a gruff voice in the unconquerable groan of the room's door hinges indicated that it had ever been an inner sanctum for Father.

Wiped as it was of his father's influence, there was one thing still true of the room, and Jonathan was almost unsurprised to be awoken from a doze on the sofa by the indefinite mutter of a deep man's voice, answered now and then by his mother's higher-pitched plaintive whine, coming from the room at the end of the darkened hall.

He went to her at once, half believing she was talking to herself, taking on Father's long-stilled voice in some unfortunate mimicry, and half excited that he might at last catch the stranger whose voice he'd so often heard from behind that door.

But when Jonathan reached the door, inches ajar and casting the yellow glow of Mother's night-lamp out into the hall, the voices ceased, and when he pushed the door open to look in, wincing as the hinges voiced his own uneasiness, Jonathan found her asleep, blue eyelids aflutter, hands crabbed like talons around the comforter's top edge.

He dared not enter, but scanned the room. When he could find nothing at all out of place, he retreated, shoulders tight, and was struck in his fleeing back by the resumption of indistinct words from the sickroom.

He surrendered to being always outside of conversation, squelched a fit of pique that his mother should carry on so, real or not.

He returned to the living room and the re-run from his childhood. On the screen, a family enjoyed an outdoor scene, the light of the sun brilliant even in black and white, their teeth catching the glint, eyes bright with joy, faces a study in shared understanding.

Once, Jonathan had hoped to have a life like he saw on television, on the shows that in his youth had promised simple pleasures: a house of his own, a wife to love, children to look up to him and wonder at his stories. What he'd gotten instead was a different kind of simple.

"You're a man now," Father had said on the day before Jonathan was to attend his first classes at the local college. He had looked right at Jonathan and not through him, his eyes taking in Jonathan's trim, strong limbs and the sharp clothes he'd bought for the next day's inauguration into the mysteries of the wider world. "And with manhood comes certain responsibilities, duties that you must shoulder without complaint and carry without faltering."

Jonathan stood before Father's desk, back straight, eyes ahead, as much of a soldier in his posture as his imagination and his father's expectations could muster.

"I'm not always going to be around to take care of Mother, Jonathan... Jack." The attempt at familiarity fell awkwardly from Father's lips, and Jonathan blushed to hear the diminutive, face hot with a sense of the forbidden, almost shamed by it. "You must promise to take care of Mother if anything should happen to me."

Without hesitation or a moment's thought, Jonathan had answered as he had imagined someone named Jack might, maybe one of those smiling boys on the old television shows. "Sure, Dad," he'd said, the heat creeping down his neck. Never before had he taken such a liberty. "Sure," he repeated, voice high and alien in his ears.

Within the year, Jonathan would come to regret his promise.

Regret's name was Sheila, and she had long, wavy brown hair and sedate, grey-blue eyes and a way of pointing out, wryly, Jonathan's peculiarly narrow view of things.

She'd been exciting in a way that glimpses of his father's past had been, had offered him a window on adventures he'd only vaguely imagined. She made him restless, caused an unnamable ache in him. They had kissed once, in the shadow of the science building after dinner and a movie, just the two of them, no fast-laughs gang to put a safe buffer between Jonathan and the girl who'd made him feel that the world might be his after all for the taking.

The kiss was warm and soft, like the late spring night around them, and it seemed to suck all sound from the world. No passing traffic noises harassed his ears, no booming bass beat from the dorm building across the quad. No drumming heart raised internal thunder.

Just that: soft lips and the silent sigh of giving in.

It was terrifying.

That feeling—uncomfortable, indefinable—combined with Mother's complaints about the time Jonathan was spending away from home "with that girl" on evenings and weekends decided the dilemma for him. Jonathan told Sheila he had to focus on his studies, suggested without saying directly that there was difficulty at home, and faded away into the dimmer regions and more remote study carrels of his small city college.

Years later, after Father's death, Jonathan kept the promise he'd made about Mother, by giving up his office job for something he could do via computer from home, turning down invitations to dinner parties and group movie outings with former colleagues and college friends. Always, he implied but never said that he had obligations. Always, there was an undercurrent in his words that was left for listeners to interpret.

Jonathan hoped his friends might think he was being mysterious rather than reclusive, that his ambiguity was inspired by a seductive secret rather than the actual facts of his mundane life.

One friend, his oldest and closest, Ron, had refused Jonathan's excuses. When Jonathan had explained that he couldn't leave Mother alone, Ron had invited himself over to watch movies or talk about the television and styles and manners of their youth. Like two much older men, they sipped overheated coffee and covered familiar ground, and it was comfortable enough and familiar enough that Jonathan felt only a little anxious at Ron's intrusion into his home.

Mother complained, of course, about the bustle and the noise of the television on the nights of Ron's weekly visits. Jonathan naturally turned up the volume to disguise whatever sounds might be coming from the sick-room, fearful that Ron might overhear the mysterious stranger at the end of the hall, even more frightened that Ron might correctly interpret words that Jonathan himself could never quite grasp.

The night that the video tape got jammed in the player, grinding everything down to an angry machine hum, Ron asked, "Is there someone visiting your mum?" Jonathan made excuses, said it was a radio program, distracted Ron with his efforts to extract the half-digested tape, and then shuffled his friend out the door with a promise to call, a promise Jonathan had no intention of keeping.

After a few days of silence, Ron called him instead. Once and then once again, and then every day for a whole month, his voice on the answering machine changing from casual curiosity to stronger concern, ending at last on an almost-angry note of desperation. Thirty days. Thirty calls. And then Ron, too, was gone, and Jonathan breathed a mingled sigh of regret at having lost his friend and relief that his friend was safe from whatever aberration had taken up residence in his house.

Jonathan's days drew steadily along, unerring in routine and tone.

The only thing that marked the future from the present was the unpredictable but definite date of his mother's demise.

Her health didn't fail her so much as she spindled it away, worrying at the loose threads in the unremarkable tapestry of her life, wishing she could start over with a basket of unused thread, bright and brilliant and eternal. The Fates had not spun what she'd wanted, and she knew the day approached when they would cut the last strand holding her to Earth.

To Jonathan, she spoke only of death, but the words she gave to the stranger, the ones Jonathan could make out when he muted the television and listened with his breath held, were of things she had always wanted to do, places she had always meant to see.

Night after night, Mother carried her flag of regret in a reverse pageant that snaked back through her life.

When she came to her childhood, her voice grew weak, and Jonathan knew she had only days left before she descended into infantile silence and then another silence more quiet still.

Jonathan recalled his father mumbling as if to boyhood chums, remembered his tone rising into that strange falsetto that had made Jonathan clench his teeth to keep from gasping aloud at the wrongness of how the stranger had unmanned him, making him once more a babbling boy.

Not much later, Mother was speaking as breathlessly as a child on Christmas morning, all high-pitched delight until he went to her door, and the stranger's voice ceased. In her son's presence, she pouted and pretended to sleep until he left again, her supper tray untouched on the bedside table.

One night, his muted television watching was interrupted by the abrupt cessation of all sound from down the hall. In the unnerving quiet, Jonathan hesitated, water in his bowels, and stared at the light glowing out from the crack in the door. He waited, heart pounding, and watched—expecting to see a shadow pass across it, even though he sensed what happened as surely as he could feel his own pulse. Mother was, of course, dead.

Jonathan peeked in and found her still and cooling, face relaxed, hands flat across her heart as though she'd pressed a sweet memory against her. Her lips were closed.

Jonathan stole a look around the room and then stepped inside, hoping that with Mother gone, the stranger might at last address him too.

There was only silence.

Once Mother was in the ground beside Father, buried on a bright spring day when the birds were intent upon spoiling his abstract grief with their chirruping, Jonathan considered what he might do.

The house was his outright, and he'd always been frugal in his spending, so he had no pressing need. He planned to give up his computer job and spend some time traveling, at last seeing the places his father had spoken of to the voice, places like Madagascar and Turkey and Morocco, names that had taunted Jonathan from the end of the hallway as words he could just make out for the sharpness of their letters and the exotic sounds of them.

He even went so far as to unearth Father's hookah from the attic and give it a place on the coffee table, where he could look at it as he watched the television, still on mute, old habits being hard to break.

When the last of the few casserole dishes had been cleaned and returned to their owners, awkward neighbors and distant relatives who had done out of duty what they might not have offered out of kindness, Jonathan sent an email with his two-week notice and sat back to let the world into his life.

For that whole day while he waited to hear back from his boss, waited for the sound of the flag going up on his email inbox, waited for confirmation that he'd at last done something toward doing something, one thought wriggled its way out of his subconscious and into the front of his mind.

Would the stranger come?

Jonathan wasn't sure what he'd do if that deep, indefinite growl came from the room at the end of the hall. He didn't know why he should expect it; Mother had been gone a week and there had been no intrusion on his lonely silence. But Jonathan thought that maybe—now that he'd declared himself ready for anything—the voice might take that as a sign.

His boss's bland reply came as the last blue fingers of sunset drew themselves backward out of the living room. Jonathan read it with a sense of growing finality, then simply turned on the television and watched the news, sound off.

A house on fire. A car bent in half around a pole. A child smiling over some small victory. Storm fronts and stock averages.

Dinner sat like a lump in his stomach as he waited for full dark, for the hour when Mother's voice would usually greet the stranger, when Father's voice had hailed his fellow with the bluster he'd always reserved for people he knew better than his son.

He was washing his dinner dishes when he thought he heard something and shut off the water, listening over the dripping of his wet hands in the sink.

There. Was that a voice?

He was halfway down the hall, hands still damp from dish soap, when the sound faded away. Jonathan gritted his teeth in frustration and turned back toward the kitchen. A step, then two, and he heard the voice again, only this time it was joined by a second, distinctly higher one.

The neighbors, Jonathan realized. It had to be. A quick check through the side door window showed a man and his son standing near the end of Jonathan's driveway, talking and gesticulating in a manner that suggested they were having an argument about something.

Inside, only silence.

Well then, he told himself. That's it.

Pretending to himself that he didn't feel the rejection, Jonathan finished the dishes, making plans in his head to find a travel agency, to buy tickets, to pack his bags.

When he returned to the television, he deliberately ticked up the volume until he could clearly hear the voices of the game show contestants guessing the clues for the round. He played along until the next show began, one he didn't like, and changed channels until he came to a nature program about wildebeests. He realized, during it, that he was straining to hear noises from the sickroom over the soothing observations of the program's mellow-voiced announcer.

Finally, Jonathan gave in and pressed the mute button. He watched dispassionately as a wildebeest kid was cut from the herd and brought down by a pack of hyenas and idly considered adding Africa to his travel plans. Just as he was wondering what inoculations he might need, he heard what he'd been waiting for all along: gruff muttering from what had once been his father's study.

Without turning off the television, Jonathan launched himself from his chair and hurried down the hall, torn between wanting to hurry and fear that the sound of his approach would scare away the stranger.

As he reached the door, pushed it open, stepped over the threshold, and flipped on the light—motions so familiar that he didn't even register them—nothing changed in the voice's volume or tone, but at once Jonathan could understand the words, every one of them.

He listened, aghast, and staggered toward the chair beside Mother's bed.

The peach bedside lamp cast a glow over the room. The quilt covering the bed was familiar, Mother's reading glasses lay on the table, the dark print of an oasis at night revealed palm trees limned in moonlight—every aspect of the room was utterly familiar, but all of it was under an alien lens with the words spilling into Jonathan's ears.

"Yes," he answered, "I do think that's true." The voice paused when

Jonathan spoke, hesitated as it considered, resumed, asking him a question.

"No, no," Jonathan hastened to assure the voice, "I agree, absolutely. You couldn't be more right."

"Do you really think so?"

A laugh.

"Whatever you'd like."

"Please, go on. Go on."

☞

Rod Serling:
An Unassuming Icon

Joe Young

Rod Serling is a name unfamiliar to many, yet if you mention the TV show *The Twilight Zone*, you can guarantee people will hum a few bars of the theme tune. The show's title is part of common parlance even among people who haven't seen it, and it has become synonymous with anything 'out of the ordinary'.

The man behind the show was also 'out of the ordinary', an undoubtedly gifted young writer driven to give the public an experience unparalleled in the world of television entertainment. In hindsight, *The Twilight Zone* could be written off as an archaic black-and-white fantasy show, which would be a big mistake; many episodes are rich in social commentary.

At the age of 24 Serling, a former paratrooper, had left the Military and moved to New York where he became a freelance writer for radio. Five years later he established himself as a TV scriptwriter with the drama *Patterns*, for which he won his first of six Emmy awards. His myriad contributions to television, an entertainment medium still in its infancy, continued to reap such awards, just a few of which are listed below.

1956 Emmy Award Best Original Screenplay:
      Patterns
1957 Emmy Award Best Original Screenplay:
1957 George Foster Peabody Broadcasting Award:
      Requiem for a Heavyweight
1960 Outstanding Writing Achievement in Drama:
1960 Hugo award for Best Dramatic Presentation:
      The Twilight Zone
1961 Outstanding Writing Achievement in Drama:
1961 Hugo Award for Best Dramatic Presentation:
      The Twilight Zone

1961 Unity Award for Outstanding Contributions
to Better Race Relations

1962 Hugo Award for Best Dramatic Presentation:
The Twilight Zone

1985 Television Hall of Fame

1988 Star on Hollywood Walk of Fame

These awards serve to validate the quality of drama created by Rod Serling and his fellow *The Twilight Zone* writers in a time when the majority of television shows were lightweight vehicles built around product placement. Sponsors had a far greater say in programming presentations than they do today, and in his early career Serling found that they refused to consider many of the topics he wanted to address in his scripts. It was not without reason that he was given the moniker 'The Angry Young Man of Television'. Passionate about the purity of his work, in 1959 he created the show for which he is most recognized.

The Twilight Zone was an anthology series with a difference, and arguably Serling's greatest achievement. It soon established him as the Shakespeare of the small screen. He realized he could get his social message across and remain within expected broadcasting policies by presenting the stories in a fantasy format. His talents was not only for scriptwriting but for recognizing the need of the show to have significantly talented and experienced writers working with him to create episodes that raised the bar for quality entertainment.

The Twilight Zone provided a wake-up call to production studios. Television could serve not only as a medium for entertainment but could also enlighten viewers, prompting people to think deeply about the context in which the fantasy was delivered. Episodes like 'The Monsters are Due on Maple Street' tap into what it really means to be human, and are every bit as relevant today as when they were first broadcast.

There have been many attempts to rekindle the series, but aside from the occasional memorable episode they have been lackluster, serving decent enough fantasy, but failing to hit the mark as modern parables. Other shows have attempted to capture the essence of *The Twilight Zone*, with only one coming close, Charlie Brooker's *Black Mirror*. With only seven episodes to date it by no means explores the breadth of subjects covered by Serling et al, but it does encapsulate the broader moral messages in a dystopian view of our potential future.

It is not without thought that I referred to Serling as the Shakespeare of the small screen; both men shared a mastery of language beyond their contemporaries, presenting us with the richness of the human condition and all of its implications horrific or comedic. Both were highly prolific, with Serling having in excess of 250 scripts to his name at the time of his death, not all of which were TZ episodes. A later show, *Night Gallery*, is less well known. Although hosted by Serling, it failed to generate as much interest in spite of having some of the major acting talents of the day involved. I think this is partly due to Serling's lesser involvement in the scriptwriting.

In spite of giving us a buzz-word for the unusual, an outstanding TV series, several other series and many scripts for radio and movies I believe his greatest gift to us is one of integrity. He firmly believed that intelligent home audiences deserved intelligent entertainment, and even his most comical scripts contain thought-provoking material.

The anthology format in which he told his stories meant there was no sense of continuation such as one would find in Star Trek or other sci-fi/fantasy offerings. For this reason, the fan base for Rod Serling's work is far smaller than those of space operas or fantasy shows in general, but it is rare to find anyone who has seen the original series of *The Twilight Zone* who has not become a fan and sought out more information on the life and work of Rod Serling.

We all owe him a debt of gratitude for showing us that excellence is possible in TV broadcasting.

☞

Less Than Nine

Amber Bierce

It wasn't the image of a limp body, wrapped in a sheet secured by duct tape, and weighed down by chains and a cement block, that bothered Nine—it was that in each visit to his dreams, that body was alive, unlike the way he had left it.

Nine knew that if he shared with his fellow inmates his recent dreams or fears, the respect he had earned as a cold-blooded murderer would shatter, despite having won the prison's honor of the most dedicated corpse sendoff.

You out of your mind? You really believe some ghost comin' back from the dead to get you in your sleep? he imagined one of the thick, muscle-bound fellows saying, barely able to keep the ridicule out of his voice before erupting into laughter. But it was *not* just in his sleep that Nine feared the ghost would come and get him.

The other prisoners would, no doubt, look at him like he was crazy, but both he and his would-be verbal torturer knew most of the men in Her Majesty's Fox Hill Prison were haunted: lips taut with suppressed screams of terror from the remnants of a paralyzing dream, eyes glazed over with the replay of life slipping away before them, stolen by their knife or bullet. Perhaps the distant memory of a beloved child's laugh, a girlfriend's grin; the images of a favorite mom-baked pie.

They all believed in ghosts.

❧

"He should hang!" used to echo between Nine's ears and pervade his daydreams, along with the image of himself hanging limp from a rope in front of a crowd watching in morbid curiosity, with individual members remarking that his eyes had started to bug out, or that they had actually heard his neck break. Perhaps marveling that even skin as dark as his could look blue.

Nine hadn't been sure about his death sentence at first—no one got hanged on the tiny archipelago of the Bahamas anymore. The justice system kept threatening to do it, but murder sentence after murder sentence went from death to life.

Supposedly, they really meant it this time—to make an example of Nine for killing Jovani—and planned to break the fifteen-year suspension. But even that threat now paled in the face of his nightmares.

At first, Nine's dreams and memories surprised him—they were delivered to him stripped of the turmoil of his last two years on the outside: highlights of friendship, flashes of making love. Barefoot walks on white-sanded beaches as the turquoise water beckoned to him and his lover.

But soon, the sand dropped away, and the beach became just the ocean, and his feminine companion turned into a tawny giant squid with hazel-green eyes treading water—a squid that simply stared at him: enormous eyes reflecting almost childlike observance, a lack of malice, and devoid of intensity.

And now, Nine's most recent dreams had taken a definite turn, with Jovani not only alive, but bent on revenge.

The first of these dreams began with deceptive innocence. In it, like previous visions, it was as if nothing had happened between the two—as if Nine hadn't stabbed Jovani twelve times, and then dumped his weighted body into an Abaconian blue hole from which he was sure the body wouldn't resurface. The dream versions of themselves were in their senior year of high school, about seventeen years old—nine years younger than the last time they had met. Jovani had no butt-length, light brown dreadlocks then—he wore his hair low-cut. Jovani had 'good hair' as the girls liked to say, although Nine could never really see it; Jovani's hair wasn't much different than his own, but Jovani's light, yellowish skin and hazel-green eyes had the girls fooled—one with such a complexion and such pretty eyes had to have pretty hair to go with it; they did not see that his parts did not match up as well as they wanted them to. Still, Jovani was good-looking, there was no denying that—and it wasn't just because of how Nine felt about him, then.

The best buds were chatting animatedly about something silly and teenaged no doubt—probably what they planned to wear on "Fun Day"—the last day of school, and the only time they would be able to wear their own clothes, instead of their stiff school uniforms—when Natasha suddenly slithered over to them. She looked so sweet, smooth, and young—her eyes wide, her smile easy; fresh and trusting. Nine felt himself grin during this night visit, aware of the dream as a dream as he moved through it, and happy to see his former lover again.

Back in those days, Nine was Lamar—Natasha had eventually nick-named him 'Nine' after enduring two periods of hospital visits to him, and hearing about his previous brushes with death. He had survived a car crash, a stray bullet, and a hit-and-run, and had come out of the womb blue, with an umbilical cord wrapped around his neck.

"You must have nine lives," Natasha had said, and the name had stuck.

Nine had liked her from the moment he saw her in tenth grade, and couldn't believe it when she'd eventually picked him over Jovani, the prince of their high school.

She and Nine had been dating a few months at that point in the dream, so when Natasha went from smiling sweetly at him, her eyes hinting that they could make out later, to seductively settling on Jovani, Nine bristled.

Then Natasha's hand suddenly cupped Jovani's crotch.

Her back now to Nine, and her hand over Jovani's growing penis, Na-tasha's thumb and fingers began to move, rendering a gentle massage.

Jovani's shocked eyes managed to stay on Nine's face the whole time, his expression, through his surprise, apologetic.

☛

Nine's grandmother used to tell him that people are at their most vulnera-ble, and wide open to possession by the spirit world, at two obvious times: when asleep, and during sexual intercourse.

She would tell the story of when she was fourteen and had been dropped off at her aunt's house while her mother had gone off to run errands. Her aunt didn't feel a need to actually watch her, since she was almost a grown woman at fourteen years old, so she made her some lunch, and then went off to take a nap.

According to his grandmother, her aunt woke up as a wolf. She snarled and growled, and as odd as the whole thing was, nearly keeping his grand-mother frozen in place in fascination and fear, when she looked into her aunt's now animal-like black eyes and saw her rearranging her body, ca-nine-like, and then on all-fours in preparation for an attack, h fled the room, closing the door behind her. She did not expect her aunt to remember how to open the door like a human, so she got help from the neighbors with her bought time. It took her aunt tearing someone's throat out for them to really believe what was happening, and figure out what to do about it.

When Nine was sixteen, his mother started telling him that sex was dangerous—that you had to be careful who you slept with, because you ended up carrying pieces of them with you forever, and vice versa. She said that you had almost-children with them, the kind that implanted themselves in various corners of your mind, the sort you didn't know were playing hide-and-seek. She said they became a part of you beyond the most basic way, that they burrowed into your subconscious, and affected the way you treated others like them; they infected your character. And since she believed the old saying about thoughts becoming words, then actions, habits, character, and then destiny, those people essentially merged with you, inevitably affecting your fate.

Nine figured the same thing probably happened when you killed someone.

❧

Nine regretted watching Jovani and Natasha have sex one evening, something Nine had done for the last time just two weeks earlier. That's when he had lost it—peeking through Natasha's window, and seeing her milk chocolate legs wrapped around Jovani's tawny, sinewy body, his buttocks clenching and unclenching as he pushed himself in and out of her. It had simply unraveled Nine as he thought about how Jovani was now a part of Natasha too, and Natasha, part of him.

❧

The second dream wasn't deceptive like the first. As Nine entered it, the air was different—thick with tension and foreboding. He and Jovani were about the same age they had been the last time they met, and again, Nine knew that he was dreaming, but he was powerless to affect it.

Nine watched as Jovani stood outside of a window he should have recognized, but he was simply an observer in the role-switch. He felt Jovani's rage and hurt as he watched Natasha and Nine make love. Jovani's chest rose and fell, and his hazel-green eyes narrowed. His mouth tightened, and his right hand balled into a fist; his left hand turned into a sheathed knife.

❧

Nine's paranoia blossomed every day—that's how he knew he wasn't crazy. Crazy was his grandaunt, Mabel, who talked to herself and god-knew-what-else, batting at unseen entities and having heated conversations with someone only she could see.

Since the nature of Nine's dreams involving Jovani had changed for the worse, it made perfect sense to him to expect an unnatural execution any holiday now. He had already figured it out: he had killed Jovani on April first—an unofficial holiday of sorts, and it seemed to set the stage for the rest of his journey. He had been arraigned on the day Americans celebrated Thanksgiving, and his own family, along with the rest of the country, also stuffed themselves: with turkey, ham, peas-n-rice, baked macaroni and cheese, salads, and pie; they appreciated a day essentially dedicated to good food, despite it not being an official holiday. Then Nine was sentenced to hang a year and three months later, on February fourteenth, another unofficial holiday of sorts. Nine figured October thirty-first was a likely candidate for Jovani's attack, or perhaps, Guy Fawkes Day on November fifth.

Nine didn't know if he preferred the advance warning, where he felt like every holiday—official or not—could be his last day alive. The previous Mother's Day, he had thought: Is this the day? Is this the last time I'll see my mother? And on Father's Day, he had wondered: Will Jovani make me hang myself today? Or frighten me to death in my sleep? Independence Day on July tenth had him thinking: Surely, J won't miss the opportunity to play with irony.

➦

In the third and final dream, Nine was himself again. He and Jovani had come to a point of catharsis, and stood facing each other in Owl's Cave Pine Forest, near the blue hole, Merlin's Lair. The air was soft with forgiveness—a triumph over a level-five hurricane.

Jovani held out his arms to him, and Nine felt relief and happiness wash over him at the offer extended. The men embraced, brotherly love and connectedness flowing through them, and wrapping itself around them like a soft blanket that soon turned into a boa constrictor. Nine then felt Jovani's weight shift, and, trapped in his arms and the leftward momentum of his body, was powerless to do anything but plunge into the oceanic subterranean pool beside them. As they descended through its oxygen-depleted depths, Nine wished in blue terror they had at least sunk feet-first.

➦

Good Friday passed, and, once again, Nine was grateful to have awakened at all.

His mother and sister usually came to see him every few weeks between them—although more so his mother.

He had told his mom about his dreams before, and she foolishly thought it was just his conscience speaking.

"Don't worry, baby, God will forgive you…as long as you're sorry," she had said, nodding her head for emphasis. Nine got distracted by the motion, thinking how odd it must be for her head to hold up her large, lavender church hat.

Nine never bothered mentioning his fears to his sister. "Ghosts can't kill you," she wouldn't say, because of the redundancy; ghosts didn't exist. She believed in only the concrete, the physical, the proven. She brushed away every family story of possession with contempt, every graveyard tale with pity for the ignorant storyteller. Latoya would not only think him silly, but stupid. Childish. Gullible.

At Christmas, both she and his mother had visited—a rare treat—bringing him a saliva-inducing plate like the Thanksgiving feast, the memory of which almost brought enough joy to combat the remnants of his fright-mares. He expected a similar feast this Easter weekend, hot cross buns and all.

He had thought they would both visit on Easter Sunday, but his sister came alone that Saturday, telling him that their mother planned to see him the next day with the full meal. She didn't say much this visit, and it didn't really matter to him that she didn't stay long—he wanted to start shoving whatever delicious food she had brought for him down his throat.

It was only after he was rushed to the hospital that it occurred to him how odd her manner was, how vacant her eyes, how there was no way the spirit staring back at him through his sister's body, was his sister.

He realized he had been fixed—the food tainted far beyond earthly poison.

As a boy he had listened wide-eyed to tales of revenge by scorned wives who anonymously gifted their husband's lover with a delicious-looking plate of food that the trollop stupidly accepted and ate. Black magic made a snake grow in her body, taking up precious space, and eating all the food she later tried to nourish herself with. Overcrowded and underfed, the girl eventually died.

As a teenager, Nine finally agreed with his sister that such stories couldn't be true—they could only be wishful thinking on the part of folks who only dreamt of having such power.

But as the eight-armed creature rapidly grew in his body, shocking and stumping the doctors trying to find a way to extricate the cephalopod from his swelling abdomen, Nine took one final look at his family members. He smiled at his mother in farewell, then through his sister at Jovani, in applauding surrender.

His stomach painted the room.

☞

Blood

Pamela Troy

It took two hours for Simona to prepare. There was her dress, one of her favorites, a midnight blue, with lace at its cuffs and two lines of embroidery on either side, from her shoulders all the way down to the hem just brushing the top of her shoes. And then she sat at her dresser as Kitra worked, the girl's nimble fingers brushing, combing, oiling, braiding and pinning, piling Simona's black hair into the elegant coif that the other wives envied. Now, sitting in the carriage with her husband, she restrained herself from occasionally reaching up to touch it.

They turned onto the grounds, and Karel gave her arm a reassuring squeeze. Herr Grossman, who sat across from them, had spent the entire ride staring at some point in the air between them. Was he a skeptic? Or was he a snob? People like that were always so high-nosed about such things, even though they were true servants rather than civil servants like Karel. No doubt Herr Grossman wore livery on formal occasions. She tried to calm herself by imagining the count's lean, gray-haired steward in a powdered wig, and only grew more uneasy.

The twilight was deepening when the carriage slowed and stopped, lamplight slanting in through the window. They were at a side entrance, of course. She had known they would never enter through the main doors, but still… At least they would not be going in through the kitchen. Herr Grossman leaned forward, his eyes focused on her husband.

"I wish to emphasize again," he said, "the necessity of absolute secrecy."

"That is understood, Herr Grossman," Karel said.

"It must be." His eyes shifted to Simona, but he was plainly not deigning to address her. "If there is so much as a trace of gossip…"

"My wife is not a gossip," Karel said.

"If there is any…"

"Herr Grossman, I do not care for the tone of this conversation. If the count had the slightest doubt about our honesty and discretion he would not have summoned us. We will return home if there are any further insinuations."

Simona looked at Karel, awed, as she had so often been in the year since they married, by this plump, round-faced man. He had dressed well for the occasion, his hair trimmed, his cheeks shaven, his moustache newly waxed. But he not only knew the difference between speaking to the count and speaking to the count's steward, he felt it. Her husband was a lion.

Herr Grossman opened the carriage door. No footman appeared. As few servants as possible would know about this meeting.

She could almost hear her mother's voice as she stepped down. "Don't gawk. Don't turn your head to stare," and so she did not look around, but she heard night birds and smelled sweet olive. Even the side entrance intimidated her, double doors that Herr Grossman opened into a golden-lit hall with a dark blue runner. And now she was on her husband's arm, following the steward down a corridor that seemed endless.

Mansur was going to be a problem. In their correspondence, Karel had already warned the count about spirit guides and about hers in particular, so perhaps the count would understand. But one never knew with the nobility. They did not have to be reasonable.

And now Herr Grossman pushed open two more double doors and they walked into a warm, fire-lit parlor. A man stood near the fireplace, his hands behind his back. A young woman sat on the sofa behind him.

Herr Grossman announced them. Simona curtseyed as her husband bowed. Then she straightened and raised her head to look at their host.

He was a tall, blond man in his forties. Like most of his class he'd been educated in Heidelberg, for he had a dueling scar—one of his high cheekbones marred by a black seam that slanted down and disappeared into his thick, yellow moustache. "Herr Perdik, Frau Perdik," the count said, jerking his head in a quick, imperious nod, not a greeting so much as an acknowledgement. "I thank you for coming."

"We are honored, my Lord," Karel said.

"I don't wish to waste time," the count said. "So I will get to the point." And here he paused, searching for words. Getting to the point seemed, for a moment, to defeat him.

Karel cleared his throat. "My Lord, in your letter you mentioned... a visitation?"

"Just so. A visitation." The count sighed, then thrust his chin in the direction of a closed door.

"In there. The long gallery. We've been seeing or hearing it for centuries. The last time before now was over thirty years ago, the week before my brother died. My late father saw it—a horseman in armor galloping down the gallery, headless, his helm under one arm." He stopped and looked coldly at Karel as though daring him to laugh. "In our family it has always portended a premature death," the count continued. "Or at least it did until now."

Again, he stopped.

"And now?" asked Karel.

"I saw it three months ago, in December, late in the evening, galloping down the gallery towards me. It passed me without a sound and disappeared through the wall at the other end. I'd heard about it, but I'd never seen it with my own eyes. And I was… My daughter, the Lady Ursula, was very ill. The doctors told me to prepare for the worst. I was concerned."

"But, as you can see," The Count turned towards the young woman on the couch. "She recovered."

Simona had longed to get a good look at the count's daughter, and now she took the opportunity to drink in every detail of the lady on the sofa.

It was no surprise that the young woman was beautiful. What plunged Simona into despair was that she had also heard she was modern and stylish. If so, she, Simona, was vulgarly, ridiculously, old-fashioned and unstylish. Lady Ursula's brown hair was pinned up simply in a round cloud that softened her large eyes and narrow, solemn face, and her pale dress hung on her gently, outlining her figure with no ruffles or furbelows, and certainly no bustle, accented only with a dark-colored shawl draped over her shoulders. Simona's coif now seemed an overdone remnant of the last century, her dress and her high collared wrap, comically outdated.

"The visitation will not leave," the count said.

"You have seen the ghost since?" asked Karel.

"I have not. But I have heard it. Its hoof beats rushed past me several times in the gallery, and I could hear the clanking of its armor. Others hear it too. Many of the servants will not enter the long gallery."

"You can't blame them for being afraid," murmured Lady Ursula.

"It kills things," the count said. "Have you ever encountered this? Manifestations with the power to injure?"

Karel glanced towards Simona and she shook her head at him.

"My daughter's little dog was the first." The girl stared down at her folded hands, nodded, and closed her eyes for a moment. "One of the housemaids found it shortly after the first visitation. The poor beast had apparently been killed and tossed into a corner of the Long Gallery. And on the patio outside the gallery, birds are found with their heads twisted almost off. A cat was killed in a similar manner. Who's to say a person will not be next? One of the servants? Or one of us? What if..." The count fell silent. He stared for a moment at nothing, then went on. "What if it is waiting for the person it wants?" he asked.

"With your permission, I must speak for a moment with my wife," Karel said.

He drew as close to her as he could with propriety, turning his back slightly to the count. "Is this safe?" he asked, his voice low. "If you have any doubts, if you don't want to do this, say the word and we'll go home."

Simona thought before answering. "I am not afraid," she said. In fact, she was afraid, but she was more afraid of admitting failure to the count. It would not help Karel's career. And how would she feel if they learned later that something had happened to Lady Ursula?

Karel turned towards the count. "I have one more question, my Lord. Was there anything different about this visitation, aside from its reluctance to leave?"

To Simona, the count looked merely like a man trying to remember, she also saw Karel's heightened alertness, the slight hardening of his eyes as he read the count's face.

"Yes," the count said. "It was an omission on my part."

Karel waited.

The count sighed. "As I have said, the visitation is not new. It has come to our family for generations, and we followed a tradition, said a prayer upon seeing it, to ensure one's entry to heaven if the worst happens. After my father encountered the visitant, he made us all utter the prayer. I said it myself on seeing the ghost this last time. After all, I am not yet an old man. It could have been coming for me." His tone brooked no contradiction.

"But your daughter did not say it." Karel said.

"I have never taught it to her. First, it seemed superstitious nonsense to me, and then when I saw the ghost, it seemed ill-omened. Go to her while she lay gasping with fever and tell her I saw the visitant? No! She is not even twenty yet." The count's eyes grew angry. "She did not gabble those words, as my poor brother did, and I thank God for it! She lives. He died thirteen years old from a fever much like hers a week after saying those words. I don't believe it is a prayer. I believe it is a curse that we have been tricked into reciting for generations!"

"But what are the words, my Lord?"

"I have no idea. They are in the old tongue, and an archaic version at that." The count rattled off, very quickly and quietly, what sounded to Simona like a rhymed couplet. Even to Simona, who knew enough of the language to negotiate with a peddler when Kitra and the cook were too busy, it was incomprehensible.

"Do you not see?" the count said. "This thing, this demon, has been denied my daughter. It refuses to leave until it has her, and I will not allow it! Never will she repeat those accursed words.

Karel thought for a moment, "My Lord, may we enter the gallery?" he asked.

The Long Gallery looked to Simona like a tunnel of darkness, its corners and angles hidden in shadow. The only light came from the fire built in a large fireplace some fifteen paces ahead of them, and a single lamp. Someone had placed a pitcher of water and a goblet on the table—no doubt at Karel's instruction—and an old helm. Where the little parlor they'd left had glinted with hints of luxury, gold and silver and brass, the gallery— lined along its length with weapons and suits of armor— hinted at a violent past. The head of a massive long-dead elk gazed down at them from over the fireplace.

"Do you sense anything?" the count asked, and Simona realized that he was, for the first time, speaking to her.

"No, my Lord," she said. The room was a little cold, but it was the chill one expected in a large, rarely heated hall this time of year. Karel helped her out of her wrap and she took the seat at the table.

Only two other chairs had been set out, and they were plainly for the count and his daughter, so Karel stood behind Simona's chair.

"The helm," the count said, once he had seated himself across from her "belonged to the ancestor who…the man who is now the visitant. The story is that he was a patricide. Do you require anything else?"

"No, my Lord." She pulled her gloves off, set them on the table and studied the helm. Dull gray, dented, lined in places with either dirt or rust. It was a less polished version of the helms she'd seen at the Kraska Museum, a metal shell to encase the head, with a slot for the eyes and a square grated window where the mouth would be. She reached out her hand and rested it against the helm, closing her eyes. For a moment there was only the feel of metal against her palm, the occasional snap of flames from the fireplace.

Whether the object she touched was a week or several centuries old, it was always the same—the images came quickly, jumbling centuries, flooding her mind with clammy visions. Shouldn't time impede it, shouldn't they... Wet green grass so fragrant, a weight lifted from shoulders and cool air against cheeks, don't turn and look back at the dark, thick poison that spreads across the ground... The banging of the helm against the rough table as the child laughs in the firelight and pounds it up and down with his soft, fat little arms, he's a strong lad, my son, and I see nothing to fear in his eyes... When here is that mass of green before me, the grass at the edge of the clearing and the broad leaves, backed by soft shadows trembling in the air... I used to play with it, yes, you can take it out of the chest, but then put it back, it was my father's, he led a long and honorable life and died in the battle of... The door opens at one end, then footsteps, and the door opens at the other end... Fancy it looks like something from a picture, but mustn't dawdle, there are rooms to clean... Thanks be to God for victory over such a thing... that empty metal slit is so restful, I'll look for a moment, letting the red from the axe spot the floor, a weight, but these boney old hands are strong... My father, yes, and human, but how could a human have taken such delight in human suffering... Nasty old thing, gave me a turn when I opened the chest, peeking up at me from among all that junk... Is tainted blood cleansed by the dew or does it defile the ground that drinks it?... Staring into that narrow blackness and thinking of the blood soaking into the beds... Well, set it out if you must, maybe someday we'll get around to cleaning it... and the door opens at one end, then footsteps, and the door opens at the other end... Not even a child's breath, only the soft sound it makes pooling across the floor, lovely like silk rubbing against silk... Kneel on the grass and utter the prayer the priest taught me, and no, I will not turn around to look I will look before me at the green, that blood cannot now touch me or my get... So bright, the hall so hot and bright and it catches so quickly... A smile like hatred congratulating itself, that was his, and I will watch for it, across the centuries I will watch... Let it glow, let it burn, let it all burn..."

Simona pulled her hand back from the helm. "Mansur," she whispered, her eyes still closed. "Shit left lying around," Mansur said. She heard the count exclaim at what had come from her lips, the rough voice of an uneducated boy.

"What does it mean?" she asked.

"What does shit mean?"

It was best not to react when Mansur was like this, so she changed the subject. "Is he here?" she asked.

"Is who here?"

"The man who rides without his head."

"He's here."

Simona opened her eyes and glanced around. There was no sign of Mansur in the darkness beyond the table. "I wish to speak to him."

"He will not speak to you."

"Why does he not leave?"

"Why do you think, you stupid bitch?"

"What are the words of the prayer? What do they mean?"

"Too late for that!"

The laughter that erupted from her jerked her so hard that her back arched, shoving the table away from her.

"Too late, too late, too late!" Mansur sang as she struggled to regain control, She could see him standing before the fireplace, a thin boy, head bent over a fiddle so that his dark greasy hair fell over his eyes, one sharp elbow silhouetted against the firelight as he sawed away at his music.

The roar began from somewhere deep within her, low at first, then rising to an inarticulate howl of anguish—not Mansur's voice, nor hers, but the voice of a man, tearing at her throat, pouring from her mouth, echoing against the walls of the hall and the ceiling overhead, and then fading, as if into some great distance.

Simona fell back into her chair, gasping, one hand at her burning throat. Mansur was gone. She felt Karel's hand on her shoulder. The count sat in his seat, his face white, but his daughter had risen to her feet, her eyes wide. "Excuse me," Lady Ursula whispered, and she turned away from the table, her footsteps echoing as she hurried away.

"We must not jump to conclusions, My Lord," said Karel, as he poured her a glass of water from the pitcher. Simona drank it down, trying not to gulp.

"That…thing…" the Count was saying. "That was its voice…it… God."

"My dear, are you recovered? What did you see?" Karel asked.

Simona set the glass down, cleared her throat. "I saw fire," she said. "I saw…I felt…people were thinking of blood." She shook her head. "It has been set out a long time, this helm, has it not?"

"It has been a fixture in the long gallery since before my great-grand-father was born," said the count.

"There is so much," she said. "So many people have seen it, have thought about it." This was always hard to explain, that she often sensed as much that was banal as was important. "Forgive me my Lord, but you mentioned the ghost had killed his father. Is it known why?"

"No," the count said. "Nothing more is known. It's said he killed his father, that is all."

"Is it said that he was punished?"

"No. He was not punished. It was a lawless era." The count turned to her husband. "Lady Ursula is… she is my only child, Herr Perdik. I know there are those who would say she is merely a daughter, but she is all that is left. I have made certain arrangements. Our name will die with me. I have accepted that, but by God, my grandchildren will live here, my grandchildren will carry on, and their children. I will not lose her. What is to be done?"

"I do not know, my Lord," said Karel. His eyes were on Simona, and she knew they would never return to the count's home. He turned to the count. "Perhaps you should learn the meaning of that prayer. There are scholars who can translate it. I know a gentleman…"

Where was Lady Ursula? Simona rose to her feet and looked around. She could feel a cool draught, and she followed that. The girl had opened one of the French doors further down the gallery, and stood there, a slender silhouette in the moonlight, leaning against the door and looking out at the garden. Shyly, Simona approached. Fresh air would dispel the iron scent of blood that hovered about her head. As she drew nearer, Simona noticed that Lady Ursula's shawl had dropped to the floor at her feet.

Simona bent to pick up the shawl and held it out to the count's daughter. As Lady Ursula reached for it, the scent of blood became a nauseating stench and Simona saw with horror that what she had thought was a shawl was a dead pigeon, its head almost twisted off, and the lady's hand was red, smeared with feathers, every window set in the stone walls of the old house is filled with orange light and the old woman walks away through the burning air of the garden, the smell of hot stones and melting metal and burning wood and boiling blood, a bundle on her back and as she passes, the old woman turns her head to smile at Simona, her chin wet with drool, a toothless version of the sly smile on Ursula's youthful lips as she murmured her thanks and draped her shawl over her own beautiful shoulders with her small white hands. Lady Ursula turned towards the garden again as if enjoying the view. But her head was tilted and her eyes were on Simona, cutting sideways at her with a cunning that made Simona think of something she had once heard Karel say. He was discussing a case that had convulsed the town, a well-regarded man, a university graduate, who one day rose early and cut the throats of his wife, her parents, and his little son.

"Moral idiocy."

Against everything she'd been taught since she was old enough to understand speech, Simona turned her back on the count's daughter without a word. She could hear her husband and the count talking, and she knew she must reach the small island of firelight where they stood. She forced herself to walk, her back straight, her footsteps steady, through the shadows, past furniture and shapes she barely noticed, her heart pounding too hard in her ears for her to hear a soft step behind her. If that shawl were to loop out over her head, twisting about her neck, snatching her back into the night before she could scream...

She stepped around a suit of armor into the light where the men were talking. Herr Grossman was nearby, waiting, no doubt, to accompany them back to their carriage. "Your good wife has returned," the count said. "I thank you, Frau Perdik, for your efforts here tonight. I hope they were not too taxing, and that you will get some richly deserved rest when you reach your home."

Karel had handed her the gloves and was putting her wrap about her. She wanted to snuggle into it, rub the high collar against her cheek and stroke its vulgar satin, but instead she drew on her gloves and looked up into the count's eyes. "Thank you, my Lord," she said, "and if I may..."

Her husband's hands tensed on her shoulders. The count had indicated the interview was over but she had to make the effort. "I believe it is very important that you translate the words of that prayer."

The count frowned. "But you, or rather, your guide, said it was too late."

"Yes, but do forgive -- I believe it is still very, very important." She did not turn to look, but she knew Lady Ursula had followed her and was standing nearby, listening.

"For your grandchildren's sake," said Simona, and she felt her cheeks grow as she spoke. "And for their children."

For a moment, they looked at each other. The count's face was blank. Something about the steadiness of his gaze made her suspect he was willing himself not to look beyond her at what stood waiting in the darkness.

"I assure you, Frau Perdik," he finally said, his voice as bland as his expression. "I will give your recommendation all due consideration."

But she knew, without putting her hand on him or anything he had touched, that he would not.

☞

Red Route

James Everington

Another of the signs went by outside, and Eliot tried to resist looking at the death count—but wasn't that number one higher than last time?

Annoyed with himself, he looked back at the road ahead. Much safer—the signs themselves were a distraction, Eliot thought—more tax payer's money wasted. The road was designated a 'Red Route', deemed especially dangerous, and regularly spaced signs showed monthly death figures for this year and last. This year's figure was higher already.

On average one person a day – Eliot could see why the road was considered dangerous for those who didn't know it as well as he. The route cut through the flat Lincolnshire countryside, but unlike the Roman-straight Fosse to the north, this road curled and snaked its way around the landscape. The signs lining its sides were written in a continuous language of zigzags, exclamation marks, and suicidal pedestrians, not to mention the ubiquitous casualty stats. And it was single carriageway all along, encouraging blind overtakings, and it ran east to west, so the sun was always in somebody's eyes.

Eliot was heading west, and through the bright fog of tiredness he was finding it hard to remember the route more than three junctions ahead. He didn't know why he felt so fatigued. He was used to the driving, but he felt curiously light-headed, unable to concentrate, not quite present. Outside, the flat countryside stretched for miles, and despite how far the eye could see, the land seemed empty too, devoid of anything for the eye to catch hold of except the stubby hedges, the arrangements of the fields, squat churches. It was summer and so sunset was slow, and Eliot found himself looking forward to the darkness that would smother the oddly desolate views around him. Only the road seemed alive, insistent, twisting itself into curious bends and curves.

Eliot sighed for what felt like the thousandth time as he approached a car dawdling in front—tourists, no doubt, meandering back from the coast. Eliot sped up—after this there wasn't another overtaking opportunity for miles. Best to go for it, to get it over quickly. He pulled out as he was thinking about whether to do it, and the white car he was overtaking seemed to speed up, as if chastened. Idiots, he thought as he passed, glancing left at them—two old dears, both looking half-dead, the old man gripping the wheel as if he daren't let go, the old woman's head slung back—asleep?

When he looked back at the road there was a car coming straight at him, lights on even in the dusk-light, blazing. Eliot screamed as it filled his vision—he flung his hands up in front of his face and shut his eyes.

He opened them—the road ahead was clear. Shaken, he pulled back into his own lane and slowed to a speed less than that of the car he had overtaken. Was he so tired that he was hallucinating? He could remember the car coming towards him, how in that last second it had looked like it was made of light.... Another of the Red Route signs went past—it was those ghoulish signs that had unnerved him! They didn't make him feel more cautious, but more fatalistic—one a day, and it was dumb luck whether it would be you, years of experience and knowledge of these roads notwithstanding.

God, I can't wait to get… home, Eliot thought, with only a slight mental pause before the last word. Get me home. The comforts of his destination seemed hard to visualise, but then he had been on the road all day. His limbs ached, and there was a twinge of pain across his chest. "I just want to lie down in the dark," he thought, as outside the cat's eye reflectors lit up in his lights. It was that time of evening when the sun was so low that it seemed brighter than at midday. And there was nothing in the flat landscape to impede its glare—"No wonder people have accidents here," Eliot thought. "Your eye is drawn outwards, looking for some elevation, some landmark to let you know that you're not somehow still where you were ten minutes ago."

The white car behind him had switched on its headlights too now, shining in his rear-view—the old man nudged forward impatiently. Eliot refused to speed up for them. His near accident, or hallucination, or whatever in hell it had been, had left him even more tense. He went past a junction with a minor road going god knew where in this countryside, and mentally ticked it off his list—past that left turning, then past a right turning a few miles later, also leading to Nowhere, then the crossroads.... He couldn't follow the route home any further than that without losing track. But he knew this road; he would remember when he got there.

Feeling more confident again, Eliot sped up so as to lose the bag of bones driving behind him, but the white car kept pace. Someone has got a bit of blood in them after all, he thought, and he looked in his mirrors expecting to see weak eyes peering over a steering wheel. But all he could see was that damn light, sunlight and headlights both, glinting and reflecting across the whole of the vehicle, and his car too. "At least dip them, you old fool", Eliot thought.

The sun was equally blinding to the front, but he still saw the red numbers as he passed them—one a day, he thought, is it really so much as that, for a single stretch of road? Three hundred and sixty-five ghosts a year added to the tally—this road must be thick with them, if only you could see them. Maybe those lights, he thought, that you think are gnats and flies in the dusk, are really the pinpricks of all the souls that died here. Eliot wasn't normally given to such brooding, but it made sense. Weren't ghosts supposed to be those who died suddenly, with deeds undone, their life's tasks incomplete? And which deaths were more untimely than those that happened at seventy miles an hour? One second routine, hand drumming along to the stereo maybe; the next your body slammed to a stop along with all the bloody energy you had thought you were in control of?

"What deeds have I left undone?" Eliot thought. "If it should be me today, then what..." But there was a myriad of things, he thought—not the horror-tale hokum of a secret untold or a will unsigned, but the normal stuff of existence left undone at the tail-end of a tired day. But then everyone...

The old man made a move to overtake him. They were about half a mile from the next right turning. "What in hell is he doing?" Eliot thought. He knew there were two tight bends before the junction. He slowed down, but when the white car pulled level it slowed down to match, so that the two cars moved in parallel. Although they were side by side, Eliot still felt dazzled by the lights of the white car; he still had to blink when he looked to his right to see what the hell...

He met the eyes of the old lady in the passenger seat, and they were dead. Open, certainly, malevolent, maybe, but obviously dead, as was the slack-jawed hang of her toothless mouth, the crazy twist of her neck. She both blazed with light and was translucent—through her he could see the old man, arms stretched for the wheel, rictus grin tight on the bloody oval of his face.

Eliot slammed on the brake, and felt his body lunge forward sickeningly before the seat-belt bit. He didn't slow to a full stop, but almost stalled, his hand automatically reaching to the gearstick to prevent this as his eyes followed the path of the bright car in front of him, still in the wrong lane and heading towards the tight corner. The light from the car was white, in contrast to the bloody glow of the low sun squashing itself flat against the land. There was a screeching sound, whether of brakes real or remembered Eliot couldn't be sure, and the white car jerked to a hideous and total stop, crumpled in upon itself, and the light that lit it from within faded, and with it the car itself.

He slammed his foot on the accelerator now, desperate to be away, to reach...home. He took the first bend at great speed but on the correct side of the road. In the rear view mirror the white car was no longer visible, and he could see nothing other than very faded skid marks. There, he thought, that's where they died and what I saw was... The sharp turn of the next bend took all his concentration to manoeuvre around, and all he could think of was the crossroads ahead. A car passed in the opposite direction, a reassuringly normal looking estate wagon with no ghost light to it, and the driver didn't even seem to notice Eliot's mad speed as he passed.

Tiredness Kills! a sign hectored Eliot as he drove, and then the inevitable Red Route sign – despite his panic he still looked at the number of deaths as he passed. "Fuck," he said quietly to himself, forcing himself to slow down to the speed limit. You're just tired, he thought, taking his cue from the other sign. It was all just a hallucination. He just had to get to his destination, straight on at the crossroads that were coming up – straight on, he could remember that now, if nothing else. Straight on, and there was no point in stopping for those pissing little roads to the left and right that led nowhere, and from which no one ever emerged. He knew this road. God my chest hurts, he thought; but then it had done all day.

He passed the sign that announced the crossroads, but he didn't slow down. Someone had scrawled something on the sign, even all the way out here, but he couldn't see what the graffiti said. The whole of the road now seemed lit up as if he was driving straight into the half-submerged sun— the red glow and the white of his own lights. He slowed very slightly as he approached the junction, but then accelerated again, for he could see in this flat and horrible countryside that nothing was approaching from either of the dead-end village turnoffs...

But then something was, a blaze stronger than mere headlights coming for and engulfing him from the left, and all at once the answers to many things—why his chest had seemed to hurt all day; why the last car he had passed had seemed not to see him; why he had been unable to remember anything beyond this junction—became clear. But not the why, the un-finished deed, for in fact Eliot could remember very little about his life. He screamed as he remembered screaming, as the bright car hit him from the side and the world turned and toppled in the blood-red sunset. This is where, he had time to think; then that light too went out.

Another of the Red Route signs went by outside, and Eliot tried to resist looking again at the death count – but wasn't that number one higher than last time?

Annoyed with himself, he looked back at the road ahead.

Mind Over Matter

Elizabeth A. Herreid

By day, Harry Wainwright was the most mild-mannered of mild-mannered mail clerks—always said "Sir" and "Miss" and "Ma'am," even when customers called him unprintable things, maintained his sweet temper in the face of the most illogical demands. When other clerks retreated to the back room, shaking with suppressed rage and unsaid come-backs, someone was bound to say, "This is a Harry situation." Off he'd go to smooth ruffled feathers, or at least to stand firm in the face of unpleasantness without returning like for like. Harry always knew how to handle the tough cookies. Hooray for Harry.

By night, Harry killed people.

Oh, not literally, of course. Call it literarily. Seated at his old Royal typewriter, he banged out stories in which characters met terrible fates with stunning regularity. These tales of brutality seemed to be the only thing he was capable of writing. He'd tried his hand at flowery poetry, attempted to write happy-ever-after fairy tales for his little niece in Boston...but darker elements always crept in. He was most contented and most successful when he was writing stories of murder and mayhem, cruelty and carnage.

He wasn't proud of it. Many of his stories shocked and disgusted him. To think that such horror could come out of his mind! Poisonings, car wrecks that left bodies too mangled to be easily identified, robberies gone wrong, whole families burned to a crisp in house fires, people pushed to their deaths from scenic overviews—he'd written them all. But horrible as they were, he found release in his writing, too. In his job, he had only the illusion of control. He was part of a massive bureaucracy, a tiny cog in a vast machine, with other cogs always ready to step in should he falter. He was a nobody, a nothing, utterly expendable. But in writing his stories, he was the ruler and creator of worlds. He could take a man from the dregs of civilization and make him all-powerful. He could take the most powerful man in the world and make him powerless, or torment him until he begged for death.

It was a heady feeling. Though he didn't care to admit it even to himself, Harry lived for that feeling.

Then came the day when, quite by chance, he forgot to bring a book to read during lunch, as was his usual routine. Bored, he picked up a newspaper someone had left on the break room table. The wrinkled, coffee-stained pages were flipped back, leading his eye automatically to a small local news article about a woman murdered a few days previously. Harry didn't normally read the news. It was one thing to write about horrors—it was quite another thing to read about them occurring in real life. But since this one had already grabbed his attention, he read it. Then he read it again.

It was, on the surface, identical to the murder in a story he'd written not two days before. The woman—a successful saleswoman for a large corporation headquartered in town—had been found stabbed to death under an overpass in an unsavory neighborhood. Almost every detail matched, right down to her hometown and the make of her abandoned car. The few details that didn't match were things a journalist could easily get wrong, especially in a rush to get a story out. Harry was torn between being pleased at the realism of his own work and an uneasy feeling that the similarities were a little too close. He shook his head, laughing at himself. What nonsense! He tossed down the paper and went back to his leftover pasta.

By mid-afternoon, he'd forgotten all about the article. It was the height of the Christmas rush. People piled in, stomping snow off their boots, leaving muddy tracks everywhere. Those with half a dozen boxes raised the ire of those only mailing one. Half the boxes had been set in the snow or mud at some point, one of which disintegrated the instant it was placed on the counter, which was, of course, automatically his fault. Half the customers hadn't applied labels, or had forgotten addresses, or ranted angrily when they learned that boxes shipped clear across the country couldn't be guaranteed to arrive in two or three days unless they paid extra. He was called a rip-off artist, a bastard, a moron, and a lackey—all in one ten minute period.

True, there were the patient customers, too—those who were prepared, waited their turn, smiled at him, said, "Merry Christmas!" when they were finished. But they seemed to be few and far between, overshadowed by their belligerent peers. By the time he got off work, footsore and drained, he wanted nothing more than a cold beverage, a sandwich, and a good long time at the keyboard.

His current story was a thriller. The protagonist had gambled his way into deep debt and in a desperate move, killed his wife for her life insurance, staging the scene to appear as if a stranger had broken in. He would have gotten away with it, but unbeknownst to him, his wife had been having an affair. She had a live video feed set up to her lover's computer—and though he didn't get to her in time to save her, the murder was seen and recorded.

Harry sat down at the typewriter and worked on the conclusion. The words came effortlessly, pouring onto the page in a steady torrent: click-ity-clickity-clack—zing! He typed furiously, the real world melting away around him as he wrote. He was there. He was part of the scene. He felt the mingled regret and horror and triumph of the killer, his resignation as his life fell in shards at his feet when the video was discovered. He felt the terror and shock of the woman's last moments, the anguished impotence of her lover as he watched the final blows fall, too far away to reach her....

At last, well after his usual bedtime, he cranked the final sheet out of the typewriter, shuffled the stack of pages together, and sat back with a satisfied sigh. He brushed his teeth and crawled into bed, his awful day redeemed.

When he arrived at work the next morning, some of the other clerks were huddled together, talking. "Can you imagine? What were the chances of the camera being left on—and pointed toward just the right spot? Wild, huh?"

Harry stopped short. He remembered the article in the paper in the break room, and icy fingers ran down his spine. He sauntered over, and as casually as he could muster, he asked, "What are you guys talking about?"

"Murder out in California somewhere."

"Yeah, guy killed his wife for her life insurance policy."

"He tried to make it look like someone broke in—"

"But he didn't know his wife had a video chat open on her computer. Her friend at the other end saw the whole thing."

Harry swallowed. "Oh," he said. He felt a little dizzy, sick to his stomach. A woman was dead. It had to be coincidence that it was so close to his story, right?

In his heart, he was already convinced otherwise. What had he done? What had he been doing all this time?

Somehow, he made it through the day. He was stupid, distracted. He entered numbers wrong, he misheard requests. Customers yelled at him even more than usual, but he hardly noticed. When the day finally ended, he rushed home, crammed stacks and stacks of typewritten pages into his old leather briefcase, and went to the library, where he would have access to the internet and to archived newspapers. He sat down with the first story—a short one about a yacht that burned and then sank—and began his search, starting with the completion date he had scribbled in pencil on the upper left-hand corner of the first page.

Locally, there was nothing on that date. He breathed a sigh of relief. But when he expanded the locations and dates, he found a similar accident off the coast of South Carolina, not two days after the date on the manuscript. The details didn't match perfectly...but there was nothing glaringly different, either.

He was sweating now. He took a handkerchief from his pocket and wiped his forehead, his hand trembling a little. He put the story back in his briefcase and, licking his fingers, withdrew the next. He checked another story. Another. For every one, he found a corresponding story in the real news: something that bore striking similarities to what he had written. At seven o'clock, when one of the librarians came to tell him it was time for him to leave, he swayed as he struggled to his feet. "Are you OK, sir?" she askedworriedlytaking in his pallor, his trembling legs. He mumbled an affirmative and shuffled out, clutching his case to his chest despite the repugnance he now felt for it.

He drove home in a daze, unlocked his front door, and stepped inside. Automatically he dropped his briefcase by the door, hung his coat, walked directly to the typewriter, fed in paper, and perched his fingers above the keys. Then he drew back in horror. What was he doing? Hadn't he done enough harm? All those people—it was his fault, wasn't it? It had to be his fault. He could never write again.

It was the most terrible punishment he could imagine. Life seemed to stretch out before him asvast grey plain, all joy drained. But what could he do about it? To write again was to risk...he hardly knew what.

He rose from his chair, removed the sheet of paper from the typewriter, and wrapped the Royal in its rubber cover. For good, he supposed. Forever. He gazed at the shadowy shape of the veiled typewriter, feeling as though his beloved had betrayed him. He hardly knew who he was without his writing. He felt lost and alone—a Harry Wainwright even he didn't know. A lump formed in his throat as he turned away and went up to his bedroom to read until it was time to turn out the lights.

➦

Ideas came to Harry with greater force than ever over the following days.

It was painful. He could have written a dozen stories that week, and it was all he could do to keep from giving in to the temptation. His only release came in the form of daydreams, letting stories play out in his mind. It was the next best thing to writing. He came up with a story about a man who clawed his way to the top until he had it all—a nice house, a great job, prestige, a beautiful wife, two little boys. Then the man was found drowned in his pool. A mystery. There were still details to work out—had he stepped on someone dangerous on his way up? Had his loving wife not been so loving after all? Harry looked forward to solving the mystery for himself. This writing-in-one's-head wasn't so bad. It was hard to keep track of all the elements, of course, but there was some satisfaction in it just the same.

He stopped by the grocery store on the way home on Friday to pick up some dinner. The place was crowded—it always was on Fridays—and only one line was open. It crawled along, people with overflowing carts stubbornly holding their places in front of people like Harry who only had a handful of items. Overhead, drippy holiday music droned on, too happy for the industrial lighting and the dingy floors. Harry let his eyes wander. He read the headlines of the tabloids—something he usually avoided, as he found them embarrassing. His eyes moved to a stack of day-old newspapers, moved over the headlines, stopped. "Television Mogul Drowned," he read. Heart pounding, he snatched up one of the copies and started reading. The man had risen from obscurity to become part owner of one of the largest networks in the nation—a household name. It was more detail than Harry had thought up, but it didn't contradict his story. The man had two daughters rather than two sons, and the speculation about the cause of death included theories he'd never dreamed up. But even so....

He felt a familiar gnawing fear in the pit of his stomach.

By the end of the weekend, he was almost frantic. He'd spent much of his time at the library, checking up on his daydreaming. For practically every story that had floated through his head he found a news story that could conceivably be linked. Even those he couldn't find gave him no hope. Not every local story made its way onto the internet. And—more sickening still—not all deaths were discovered immediately.

And yet he couldn't stop thinking of new scenarios, new stories, new plots. His mind ran away in spite of him. He tried to read, but that only made his imagination more active. He tried to watch TV, but his mind wandered—took off on tangents based on what he was watching. He paced the worn rug in his living room, pulling at what was left of his hair, groaning to himself. He had to stop thinking. It was one thing to give up writing, but how could he possibly keep his thoughts focused at all times? Or did the answer lie in the other direction—to blur and muddy his thoughts until he could no longer come up with new ideas?

With that in mind, he drove to the liquor store. He entered the place timidly—he wasn't a drinking man as a general rule, and couldn't remember the last time he'd bought anything harder than beer. Just walking into the store made him feel vaguely dirty. The plethora of brands and bottles dazzled him—so many exotic names and oddly shaped containers, so many varieties of sweet release. He selected an inexpensive rum and checked out nervously, fumbling, dropping his money as he tried to pay. He was intensely aware of the squinting, suspicious gaze of the tattooed clerk. His mind wanted to build a story around this store and the man who passed him his change, but he wouldn't let it. He snatched the paper bag-cocooned bottle from the counter and rushed out.

Peering through the frosty windows of Harry's little house twenty minutes later, one would have found him seated at the kitchen table sipping rum—blinking as it burned his throat—with an earnestness that might have been comical if not for the panicked desperation in his eyes.

He awoke the next morning with the first hangover he'd had in years, knives stabbing the backs of his eyeballs, stomach churning. He didn't remember much about the night before. Surely that meant he'd been successful. But how to go on from today? He couldn't keep this up forever.

He stumbled out of bed and showered. It was still early, so on a whim, he walked the two blocks to the nearest grocery store and bought a newspaper and a cup of the terrible coffee they sold by the register. It smelled like stale cigarettes, but it was hot and caffeinated, and he forced it down despite his stomach's protestations as he walked home again, reading the paper as he went.

The front page story was about a driver who jumped a curb and killed two kids. It seemed familiar in a vague sort of way, but with all the bad news in the world, didn't it all start to sound familiar? Despite that logic, through the pounding pain in his head came the uneasy feeling that just because he didn't remember the night before didn't mean he hadn't been thinking at the time. No matter what he did, he wasn't safe. Even in sleep, who was to say his dreams couldn't reach out and strike?

When he got home, he poured himself another drink to steady his nerves. He called work and said he wouldn't be in—something personal had come up. He paced, bit his nails, paced, thought—stopped himself thinking. Finally, he uncovered the typewriter one last time, and sat down.

Officer Stan Trevor leaned against the wall of the entryway. "Hey, Brian," he said to his partner. "Did you hear about the suicide note?" He shifted his wad of gum to his other cheek with a twist of his tongue. "Guy thought all his bad thoughts came true—like if he imagined a murder, it'd happen somewhere."

Brian stepped in out of the bright winter day, blinking in the sudden dimness. "Man."

"Yeah. Imagine having that on your conscience. You can kind of understand why he did what he did. Guess he wasn't in his 'right mind', as they say. At least maybe his family can find some consolation in that."

Brian shook his head with a sigh. He peered into the silent study, at the shrouded black typewriter and the heaps and heaps of paper yet to review. He stepped in just far enough to bend over and read the top sheet of one of the stacks. "This one's about a little girl who sets the house on fire in the middle of the night while her parents are arguing upstairs. Hey, isn't that what they think happened to your—"

"Yeah," Stan interrupted. "Just a coincidence, of course." He glanced at the typewriter and shivered. "All the same, let's wait outside. Place gives me the creeps."

Last Man's Club

Arthur Carey

The grating, metallic ring of the doorbell dragged George Daume from a fitful nap. He jerked back the handle of the duct-taped vinyl recliner and struggled to his feet. Across the cluttered living room, a small TV murmured, and Oprah smiled at the camera. Daume limped to the front door.

A man in brown cap, brown shirt, and brown shorts shivered in the March wind. "Package," he said. "Sign here."

Daume scrawled his signature and carried the package inside. He walked through the living room and into the tiny kitchen, banging open drawers until he found scissors.

Inside the wrapping he found a piece of paper atop a mass of plastic bubble wrap. "Mr. Daume," the note read, "before dad passed away at the Veterans Hospital in Albany, N.Y., last month, he asked me to send you this. He said you'd understand." It was signed Edward Arkin.

Arkin...Arkin... An image formed in his mind--a freckled young man with uneven teeth.

As he cut through the bubble wrap, Daume suspected he knew what the package contained—a bottle of wine. He was right. He unwrapped the bottle and set it carefully on the scarred Formica kitchen table. The cork, pitted and crumbling, had blackened with age. A corner had been torn off the label, but he could still read the faded pencil marks: Neally, Simpson, Crosetti, Sloan, Arkin, Daum. The "e" in his name had vanished. He squinted at the date: A... ust 14, 1944.

Arkin...

Arkin had been the kid in their squad in the 1st Infantry Division, the Big Red One. Mostly draftees, they had fought—and sweated—and bitched—through the hedgerows of France after the Normandy invasion. He picked up the bottle, cradling it in arthritic hands, the veins dark and distended like the tributaries of a swollen river. He recalled the bottle contained red wine. Burgundy? Cabernet?

The bottle had survived unbroken in the cellar of a stone house damaged by artillery fire outside Villeau. His under-strength squad had taken shelter there—Richards, balding and serious, the only married man, who wound up being dubbed Pappy; Sgt. Sloan, the tough, foul-mouthed squad leader who had joined the Army during the Depression for three hots and a cot; Crosetti, a wise-cracking bartender from Chicago; Simpson, from Ann Arbor, Michigan, a kid just out of high school like himself; Neally, a beefy, tattooed longshoreman, and Arkin, the platoon's wiry medic.

They salvaged the unbroken bottles.

"Belly up to the bar, boys," boomed Crosetti. He dug out the cork with his knife and began sloshing wine into dented canteen cups, ignoring Simpson, a teetotaler.

"What are we drinking?" asked Arkin suspiciously.

"Who cares?" grunted Sgt. Sloan.

When the bottle was empty, Crosetti tossed it into a corner and laughed at the dull explosion that followed. "Ka Boom…just like a Kraut potato masher!" More bottles were emptied and followed the first into the corner, lobbed like hand grenades. Finally, only one remained intact. A tipsy Pappy rescued it from Crosetti, ignoring his protests.

"No, let's save it," he insisted. "Leave it for the last man, like they did in World War I."

Pappy pulled out a stubby pencil and printed the date on the label in heavy black letters. Underneath it, he scrawled his name. The others followed. "I'll hold on to this," Pappy said. "If the bottle makes it through the war, the last guy dodging the repo man can lift a glass to the others."

The repo man. That was how they referred to death. It was all over for you when the repro man showed up to repossess whatever you had—your car… your furniture… your life.

Daume looked at the bottle as if it were a rare antiquity unearthed at an ancient burial site. He remembered Pappy wrapping the bottle carefully in a brown G.I. towel and stuffing it deep within his pack.

Miraculously, the bottle survived the fighting in France and the long slog through Germany. Pappy didn't. A mortar round had cut him almost in two in fog-shrouded woods on a frosty winter morning. Neally became custodian of the bottle. He still had it when the war ended.

Daume became a long-haul trucker, marrying a pretty telephone operator he met at a dance. They had lived contented but childless until her fatal stroke three years ago. He avoided the Big Red's reunions and the

1980s movie. The Christmas cards dwindled over the years, and he lost track of his squad mates, except for Arkin, the self-appointed secretary of the group. Arkin kept him up to date.

Simpson, a two-pack-a-day man, had escaped some of the final push into Germany when a shell fragment sliced off his left index finger, and he had been invalided home. He died of lung cancer in the 1960s.

Daume looked out the window at the gathering dusk. Who else.... Oh, yes, Neally. Neally had become a successful plumbing contractor in Seattle. He suffered a heart attack on a golf course in Scotland in '83... or was it '84? Crosetti acquired the bottle and passed it on to Arkin before entering a hospice with pancreatic cancer in '93. Sloan? Sloan had simply vanished. And now Arkin was gone.

☛

Daume studied the bottle. Probably tastes like crap after all these years. The wine, murky and mysterious behind the dark glass, called out to him. How could he not open the bottle? Didn't he owe it to the others? Their faces surfaced again, frozen in his memory like images in a Civil War Daguerreotype. He had to open the bottle. But he didn't have to drink it.

Daume rummaged through a drawer and found a corkscrew. He rarely drank. Medication and alcohol were a bad combination. He ignored the array of small white pill containers that lined the kitchen counter like miniature plastic tombstones and got a juice glass out of a cabinet above the sink.

The cork rose with protest, emerging with a sigh. A tart, acid aroma wrinkled his nose.

Daume filled the glass with wine. He took a sip and then another. His eyes watered, and he swallowed the bitter liquid with difficulty. The four walls of the kitchen wavered and collapsed without warning. He drifted, powerless, a swimmer overtaken by a swiftly flowing current....

☛

"Incoming!...Incom..." Noise and pressure and fire swallowed up the warning. Daume cowered in the shallow foxhole, eyes shut. He opened them to see the world convulsing in a sea of red and yellow flame. He heard a voice. His own? Arkin's? "Sweet Jesus... Oh, Sweet Jesus..." Then the voice and the light melted away. He coughed in the thick, gray fog of smoke and dust and looked up.

Sgt. Sloan, eyes red marbles in a blackened face, loomed over the foxhole. His lips moved but Daume was trapped in a world without sound. "Wha... What?" He shook his head, which seemed stuffed with cotton, to clear it.

"Whump, whump"…The repetitive thud of American guns replying to the Germans broke the silence. Sloan's voice forced its way into his head. "…damned 88's! On your feet before the Kraut artillery opens up again."

Daume shoved the form next to him. "Get up, Arkin!" But Arkin didn't move. Daume jerked back Arkin's arm, the one with the red cross on the white armband. Blood welled at the base of Arkin's neck, oozing below the protective rim of his shredded steel helmet.   Daume looked up frantically. "He's dead, Sarge! Arkin's dead!"

"I can see that," said Sloan, his voice gone flat and bitter. "Pull one of his dog tags and haul your butt out of there before we both join him."

Daume struggled to his feet. He looked at the back of his hands, smooth and marked only by dirt. Where were his glasses? This is wrong. Arkin shouldn't be dead. I shouldn't be here. What's going on? Sloan's impatient face offered no answers. Then the gray sky dissolved, and darkness embraced him like an eager lover.

☛

A woman's voice, shrill and insistent, jerked him back to the present. On the tiny TV screen in the next room, Oprah listened sympathetically to a blonde with hatchet-sharp features and close-cropped hair. Daume shook his head to clear it. The wine! It must be the wine! Somehow it had dragged him back to the past, but it was a different past from the one he'd experienced!

For a moment, he saw the squad again, his brothers in arms—dirty, sweaty, unshaven, almost indistinguishable in dented steel helmets, muddy boots, and filthy fatigues. Most were like him--young and unsure, ground down by fear and exhaustion. And yet he had never lived life so fully as during the war, greeting each new day as an unexpected treasure.

As if a switch had been flicked, fragments of memory surfaced: Sloan's orders, delivered in a laconic, southern drawl, Crosetti's endless dirty jokes, the slender, dark-haired woman in the photo that Pappy preserved in his helmet liner, Simpson's pale schoolboy face and Bible reading, and Neally's constant bitching. Daume felt like crying. He had lost a family he'd never realized he had.

He looked at the half-empty glass and sniffed the contents reluctantly. The bitter fumes burned his nose. He took another slow, cautious sip. The room turned into a gray funnel, and he plunged down it.

☛

A fuzz-cheeked lieutenant lowered field glasses. Then he slid, fanny first, down the slope, dislodging a minor landslide of sand and rock on the men waiting below. "Sergeant!"

Sloan stubbed out a cigarette and pushed wearily to his feet. "Yessir."

"The field is clear up to the farmhouse," the officer said. "Form up your squad. We'll reconnoiter single file abreast. The rest of the platoon will provide cover."

The boyish lieutenant's Adam's apple vibrated like a chicken's when he was nervous, which was most of the time. He had taken command of the platoon three days before, and his crisp, shiny field jacket still had creases down the arms.

"It might be better to put one man out on point, lieutenant, with the rest of the squad farther back," Sloan rasped.

The officer's lips tightened. "We'll do it my way, sergeant."

Sloan turned to the squad. "Form up on the top of the slope, people." Under his breath: "Asshole ninety-day wonders!"

"What was that, sergeant?"

"Nothing, sir."

Across the field, the two-story stone farmhouse appeared lifeless. No smoke curled from the chimney. No chickens or dogs wandered about. Daume looked around. They were all there—except Arkin. He shivered in the warm July sun.

"Cripes," whined Neally, appraising the barren ground, which had been disked for planting and then abandoned. "There ain't no cover at all. That butter bar better be right about no Krauts bein' in there."

They set out across the field, the squad spread out in a thin line with the lieutenant on the left, Sloan on the right. Daume clutched his M1 rifle. They were a quarter way to their goal when flashes of light winked in an opened upstairs window of the farmhouse. Daume froze.

"Machine gun!" cried Sloan. Daume, on the right side of the file of advancing infantrymen with Crosetti and Neally, hurled himself to the ground. Simpson, Pappy, and the lieutenant, off to the left in the sweeping arc of fire, had no time. A metal rain scythed them to the ground like stalks of wheat.

"Back! Pull back!" screamed Sloan.

Daume rolled over, dug his elbows into the soft earth, and crawled, crablike, to the rear. He focused on the bottoms of Sgt. Sloan's boots and followed them blindly. When he reached the safety of the slope's reverse side, he looked back. Pappy and Simpson lay crumpled where they had fallen. Next to them, an expression of shock on his face, lay the lieutenant, his uniform finally dusty. Daume shut his eyes and reopened them. The

sun slid behind a cloud, and shadows swept over him.

He jerked awake. On the television, a camera panned across the studio audience. Oprah was back. The picture flickered as a fresh gust of wind rattled the antenna on the roof.

The wine's aftertaste was bitter as ashes. Reaching for the pencil he used for doing newspaper crossword puzzles, Daume drew ragged black lines through the names of Arkin, Pappy, and Simpson. He sank back in the chair. What happened to the rest of them? The wine beckoned to him again, dark, mysterious, foreboding. Daume's hands trembled as he refilled the glass and tipped it back… back…

"Whatta dump," Neally griped. He kicked a broken chair out of his way and stepped into the ruins of the cottage. Broken pottery and smashed furniture littered the floor. Wind whistled through cracks in a shell-splintered wall.

"At least it's out of the rain," said Sloan.

"So when do we get some replacements, Sarge?" groused Neally.

"Who knows?" Fatigue dulled Sloan's voice. "May not be for a while. Division's taken a pounding."

"Tell me about it," replied Neally. He leaned his Browning against a wall and glanced around. "Whoa! Looky, looky at what's in the corner…a German flag." Rain tattooed the thatch roof. Daume's eyes, growing accustomed to the gloom, registered a torn red rag with a black swastika crumpled in a corner.

"Don't touch it," warned Sloan. "Krauts been booby-trapping crap like that."

Neally looked at him incredulously. "Are you kiddin'? That's worth $20 or a bottle of scotch to some jerk-off in the rear." He walked over to the flag and bent over it.

"Dammit, Neally, I said…" Sloan began.

The blast that interrupted his words sent the sergeant and Crosetti crashing into a wall and knocked Daume to the floor. When he dragged himself to his feet, ears ringing, Sloan was bent over the bloodied remains of Neally.

The rain had stopped. A scattering of stars, cold, pure, far removed from death and destruction, appeared through the torn roof. Daume gazed at them in wonder as they drew him, unresisting, to their light.

He blinked and the kitchen swam into focus. Oprah had gone to commercial. He wanted to hurl the wine bottle across the room. Arkin…Simpson…Pappy…now Neally. All gone. Only Sloan and Crosetti remained. If they died, what about him? Would he cease to exist? Did he exist? Maybe he was a bit player in some higher power's drama, a pawn in an invisible board game. His stomach lurched as he drew a line through Neally's name. Which world was real? Which was false? There was only one way to find out. He poured more wine into the glass and drank, eyes watering. Once again, the world imploded, sucking him down a black hole.

"How many do you want, kid?" Crosetti demanded impatiently. In the lantern's light, he appeared ferret-faced--jaw angular, ears rounded, eyes bright.

Daume studied the smudged, greasy cards. "Two."

Crosetti smirked. "Hoping the kicker will give you a second pair, huh? Suckers never learn." He threw two cigarettes onto the pile on the rumpled brown blanket. "Raise two."

The two new replacements—Daume hadn't bothered to learn their names—had dropped out.

Sloan shook his head and threw in his hand. Daume studied his cards. The two he had drawn lay hidden behind two sevens and a king. He uncovered one card. A three. He peeled back the last card. It was a seven.

"Well?" prodded Crosetti. "You in or out?"

Daume tossed two cigarettes onto the pile and added three more. "Raise you three."

Crosetti grunted and tried to read Daume's face. "What you got, kid? Two pair?"

"Pay up and find out."

Crosetti hesitated and threw five wrinkled Lucky Strikes onto the blanket. "See your three and raise you two."

Daume studied Crosetti. Crosetti's eyes didn't waver. A faint smile touched the corners of his mouth and vanished.

Daume didn't know whether or not his hand was good enough to beat Crosetti's. But he sensed the shape of the future beyond this hand, this game, this night. Somewhere down the line, Crosetti would draw his last card, and it would be the ace of spades.

How long do you have to live, Crosetti? What's waiting for you? A bullet? Shrapnel? Or will you step on a Bouncing Betty? And how long does

Sloan have? How long do I have?

He tossed in his cards face down. "Your hand."

He was wrong about Crosetti, though. Crosetti wasn't the next to die. Sloan was. Sloan, who had escaped death in the desert in North Africa before Daume joined the unit…Sloan, who was cautious, competent, and experienced… Sloan, whose luck ran out just like all the others.

The rest camp with its clean sheets and hot showers had faded from memory as they slogged down a nameless road in Germany, twin columns of silent men almost lost in a gray shroud of sleet. In the churned up center, a stream of trucks, jeeps, ambulances, and tanks ploughed by, splattering the frozen marchers.

As daylight faded, the driver of a 1 ½-ton Chevy truck who hadn't slept in two days jerked awake and hit the brakes to avoid rear-ending the vehicle ahead. His truck, pulling a 105mm howitzer, swerved sideways in the slush, striking four soldiers in the left-hand column of marchers. Three suffered broken bones and were evacuated to the rear. The fourth, Sgt. Sloan, died on a dirty shelter-half spread beside the road, without regaining consciousness. Daume collected another dog tag. It read: CLARENCE R SLOAN 37347556 T42 43 O. He looked up in the cold falling dusk and imagined himself on a roller coaster that had lurched, slowly, relentlessly, to the highest point of the track. And then the rails fell away beneath him and he plunged down…down….

☛

Oprah was gone. In her place was a quiz show with a giant spinning wheel. Daume turned off the TV. He returned to the recliner, glass in hand, and closed his eyes. Arkin…Simpson…Pappy… Neally…and now Sloan. All gone. Only Crosetti remained—and himself. Who would be the next to die? He drew a shaky line through Sloan's name, refilled the juice glass with wine, and drained it. And then he waited.

☛

Moonlight dappled the meadow that lapped at the rocky flank of the low hill. Daume tried to cut through the fatigue that fuzzed his mind. Safe in the forest, he studied the hill for movement…a glint of metal…underbrush that seemed out of place…a white face…He looked with the wary eyes of a veteran for clues that might keep him alive.

With two new stripes on his sleeves, he was responsible for the three soldiers kneeling behind him. Only Crosetti's face was familiar. Daume frowned at the pockets of dark shadow spilling down the hill and across the meadow.

"Too quiet," he grunted.

Quiet didn't mean safe. Daume's patrol was looking for pockets of resistance left by the retreating Germans. He eyed the scrubby slope distrustfully.

"Okay," he said at last, "Crosetti, you and I'll take a look. We'll leave the greenies here to support us. "

Crosetti shook his head. "Four targets make for better odds than two." When the argument failed, he fell in beside Daume, grumbling. They edged cautiously out of the protection of the trees and started zigzagging across the meadow, Daume on the right, Crosetti on the left.

☛

On the hill, Lance Corporal Franz Kuebler burrowed deeper into a shallow depression shielded by thick grass. His bladder threatened to burst. He cursed his forgetfulness in not bringing a bottle in which to relieve himself. Kuebler was 19, a veteran of the German Army's painful retreat into Germany. If the enemy appeared, he intended to take one shot and withdraw quickly before he could be flanked and pinned down. He rubbed his eyes. Movement! At the edge of the wood, 300 meters away, two brown blobs bobbed up and down. He pushed the K98 bolt-action rifle aside and peered through battered field glasses, their eyepieces worn bare. He adjusted the focus. The blobs became helmets.

Ami—American soldiers! Kuebler put down his field glasses and picked up the rifle. He no longer thought of dispatching the enemy as killing. It was just a job, one to be performed efficiently and forgotten. He squinted through the scratched 4-power scope. Was one of the patrol an officer or a noncommissioned officer? Hard to tell. Still, it should be an easy kill in the moonlight. He swung the rifle from right to left and back, debating which of the moving figures to target first. He selected one and squeezed the trigger.

Crrackk … a flat sound tore the night. Kuebler pulled back the bolt smoothly to eject the round, chambered another, peered through the scope, and fired again. Crrackk…

A sharp blow to his helmet knocked Daume from his feet. Black dots, swirling like snowflakes, filled his vision. Suddenly, he was on the roller coaster again. Gravity betrayed him, and he dropped, headlong, into a familiar void.

☛

He jerked upright, the room spinning. Sniper! A sniper got Crosetti. But I'm still here! His head pounded and he breathed deeply, fighting the impulse to vomit. Daume stared at the wine bottle in disbelief. The level rested well below the label.

He rose, wincing as a sharp pain from his bad knee penetrated the anesthesia of the wine. Darkness had fallen outside, and the wind had tailed off into fitful blustering. He switched on a light. The kitchen's ugliness, masked by daylight, revealed itself in the harsh brightness. He didn't feel much like eating these days. He suspected the recurring sharp pain in his stomach was more than indigestion, but he was afraid to go to a doctor and find out.

Daume picked up the bottle and limped to the sink. He started to pour out the wine. The thick, black stream flowed over the chipped sink, pooling at the drain.

No! He tipped the bottle up before the last of the wine escaped.

Daume stared at the disfigured label. Only two names remained legible, Crosetti's and his own. He picked up the pencil with a shaking hand and obliterated Crosetti's faded signature.

How would it end for him? Perhaps it wouldn't end at all. Perhaps that was why he sat alone in a dirty kitchen, the sole survivor of fate's relentless zeroing out of the squad's existence. But he had to know. He raised the bottle to his lips and drained the last of the wine. The universe contracted. He was swept away again, a solitary voyager set adrift without a compass on the uncharted, unexplored sea. This time without a way home.

☞

Black Mirror:
Season One

Joe Young

I'm always wary of modern TV shows which allegedly have a Twilight Zone vibe, mainly because since the original black-and-white series there have been many attempts to duplicate the quality and style in contemporary settings. No one has succeeded, not even under the guidance of the original studios until Zeppotron produced Charlie Brooker's *Black Mirror* which aired in the UK on Channel 4 in Dec. 2011 and ran for three seasons ending with 'White Christmas' (Season 3, Episode 0) 16 Dec. 2014. All three seasons available in both DVD and Blu-Ray format on region 2 (B) only.

Black Mirror perfectly encapsulates the concept of The Twilight Zone. In Brooker's words: "Each episode has a different cast, a different setting, even a different reality. But they're all about the way we live now—and the way we might be living in 10 minutes' time if we're clumsy."

Finding the right story to start an anthology series is a difficult task, however in the case of *Black Mirror* there isn't a single episode which wouldn't have been suitable.

Pilot episode 'The National Anthem' tells of the kidnapping of the new 'People's Princess' Susannah (Lydia Wilson) and the bizarre ransom expected to be fulfilled by Prime Minister Michael Callow (Rory Kinnear). Although the core demand appears frivolous, it is a perfect introduction to a dystopian society in which anything is possible. This is sharply observed satire taking a preposterous notion and making it creepily real, presenting it as the next logical step in society's evolution—if we are not careful.

In a truly life-or-death situation, the tension has been built flawlessly by all members of the cast including the cutaway vignettes showing the public's ever-changing reactions to the events as they unfold.

In the true spirit of The Twilight Zone, this episode shows the width and depth of humanity in broad artistic strokes and pulls no punches when showing how dispassionate we are to the plight of others, indeed indulging an ever present sense of schadenfreude.

➡

The second episode, '15 Million Merits,' is an indictment of the world of talent shows, successfully building a possible future scenario in which talent shows are seemingly the only way to exit the rat race. The visual elements of this episode are presented as commonplace, but the layered plot is deep enough to display the grip so-called 'entertainment' has on us.

'15 Million Merits', has no problem showing the viewer something new. By advancing the current trend of banal talent shows to the nth degree, Charlie Brooker employs aspects of Science Fiction to great effect. As society becomes ever more tolerant of the whims of TV moguls, the stranglehold on our future gets tighter.

Bingham Madsen (Daniel Kaluuya) has the fifteen million merits described in the title. These merits pay for everything including an audition to appear on the talent show 'Hot Shots.' However Bingham, rather than using the credits for his own benefit, generously buys an audition ticket for singer Abi (Jessica Brown Findlay). Despite her obvious singing ability, Abi is forced by the judges' panel (Rupert Everett, Julia Davis and Ashley Thomas) into a wholly different profession. Bingham then works to again earn fifteen million merits so that he himself may audition. His performance is completely unexpected, leading to an ending which I for one did not see coming.

➡

Episode three's story 'The Entire History of You' has been acquired by Robert Downey Jr's production company. Hardly surprising as it is one of the most damning criticisms of social media I've ever seen.

In this futuristic story, everyone has a small gadget, 'the Grain,' surgically implanted behind the ear. Its function is to store your memories, which can then be played back within your own head or on any compatible device. Although several steps beyond YouTube, Facebook, and Twitter, it presents an impending reality.

Liam (Toby Kebell) is afraid a recent work appraisal may have gone badly, but the Grain allows him to replay the appraisal for others to watch and discuss. He's pestered to do that at a dinner party hosted by one of his wife Fion's (Jodie Whittaker) friends, but is spared the embarrassment by the host, Jonas (Tom Cullen). Later, when replaying the events of the evening, Liam spots indications that Fion has been unfaithful.

The Grain's technology plays back video of every event you experience. This is an idea which has truly frightening potential in a society in which we routinely distribute the minutiae of our lives across social media. It is only a matter of time before such technology destroys any privacy we once had.

In summation, *Black Mirror* has proven to be excellent in all aspects: setting, characterisation, and morality. If you have not already seen it, you are truly missing out.

☞

Black Mirror:
Season Two and the Christmas Special

Joe Young

Season 2 of the *Black Mirror* horror/science fiction television series begins with the episode 'Be Right Back' in which technology provides a solution for the ultimate tragedy.

Ash (Domhnall Gleeson) and Martha (Hayley Atwell) are an instantly likeable young couple. When Ash is killed, grief-stricken Martha accepts her friend Sarah's (Sinead Matthews) suggestion of a phone app that collates all Ash's online information and simulates his voice and mannerisms, enabling Martha to interact with a virtual version of him as if he were alive.

The simulation then becomes even more realistic with the addition of an upgrade. At first, this fulfills all Martha's needs, but—as is the way with these cautionary tales—things soon go wrong. Sad in its ultimate revelation, this episode appears to be less about our technological future and more about our reliance on surrogates for answers they truly can't provide.

The second episode, 'White Bear', mixes a subject seldom covered in genre films and series with a second more common theme: that of the societal breakdown shown as entertainment such as in 'Series 7: The Contenders' and Stephen King's 'The Running Man'. The first subject I will not comment on as it provides the twist in the tale. This is probably the most gruesome episode across all seasons, with a truly bleak ending.

Victoria Skillane (Lenora Crichlow) is an amnesiac; she awakens in a chair with obvious signs of having attempted suicide. Around her, she sees images of a young girl, yet no one else is present. When she ventures outside, pedestrians begin filming her with their mobile devices. She cries out for help, but everyone just keeps filming with their cellphones.

A car pulls up and a man (Michael Smiley) gets out carrying a shotgun.

He fires at Victoria, misses, and gives chase as she runs for her life.

'White Bear' transcends the genre, never missing a beat with the brutal nature of the story. Not all is as it appears in this tale which has more twists than a corkscrew. The ending in particular is outstanding in its simplicity. Of particular note is Lenora Crichlow, whose acting elevated this episode beyond expectation.

The final episode is called 'The Waldo Moment'. It turns us full circle back into the world of politics. Jamie Salter (Daniel Rigby) is a disillusioned comedian using performance-capture technology to play a blue cartoon bear named Waldo, a comedy foil used to interview the politically powerful.

What initially could come across as a cross between Ali G and the Bo Selecta Bear takes a much more sinister turn when show producer Jack Napier (Jason Flemyng) uses Waldo to harass Conservative candidate Liam Monroe (Tobias Menzies) before deciding to run in the election against him.

The overall tone is one of subversion, and this episode presents a future in which—if we're not careful—we could one day have a whole new type of puppet government controlling the country.

The Christmas special, 'White Christmas', covers the darker side of human nature and foreshadows a disturbing new technology. This interwoven triptych, starring Jon Hamm and Rafe Spall, touches on our most basic desires for love, acceptance, family, and justice.

Matt Trent (Hamm) is a somewhat suspect 'life coach' helping shy men to chat up women. This he achieves live via 'Z-Eye' technology, effectively logging into someone else's head in order to see through their eyes. He can then relay tips and techniques to them like a futuristic Cyrano. When one of his clients gets in over his head, Matt is plunged into a nightmare in which his only hope for redemption rests with the enigmatic Joe Potter (Rafe Spall).

The ending truly justifies the means in this story and perhaps provides the most chilling finale of any of the episodes to date.

Charlie Brooker has succeeded in bringing morality tales back to our screens without being preachy. Of all seven episodes, there hasn't been one in which the acting or production values has fallen below excellent. This series has exceeded the legacy left by The Twilight Zone, and I sincerely hope for a third series.

Lightning Source UK Ltd.
Milton Keynes UK
UKHW010714270223
417728UK00001B/71